The Property Process

A step-by-step guide to understanding the process of buying a property

Sheryl Sebastiao

Acknowledgments

This book is dedicated to my late father. Thank you, Dad, for teaching me to never give up. Thank you to God and all my family and friends, including my amazing mum, husband, and my daughters, and four special people; Temi, Jane, Lucky, and Esther, for their encouragement and constant support. The early mornings, the long days and late nights were worth it, and I am immensely grateful to you all.

Disclaimer

The information provided throughout *The Property Process* is not, and never intended to be taken as financial investment advice, legal advice, or otherwise. Though care has been taken to ensure the information is correct at the time of writing this book, Sheryl Sebastiao cannot take any responsibility for any oversights and consequences as a result of using this information. Property investment is a risk, and any individual who chooses to make an investment based on the information provided should always seek professional independent, financial advice before deciding to invest. The Property Process does not guarantee homeownership, nor does it provide any financial or legal advice as the author is not qualified to do so. All information provided is for educational and illustrative purposes only.

Published by Authentic Worth

Printed in the United Kingdom

Website: www.authenticworth.com

Email: authenticworth@gmail.com

ISBN NUMBER: 978-1-8382179-0-7

Contents Page

Introduction

Buying a property for most people is one of the biggest financial commitments they will ever make in their lives. Owning a property becomes a goal for many people at some point, yet, knowing what to expect during the process, and understanding the different stages, so that informed decisions are made, can be difficult.

The Statista Research Department via the **Statista.com** website found that:

"Younger potential first-time buyers between the ages of 18 – 40 in the United Kingdom (UK), owning their own home is their top life goal. Respondents to a Santander survey on potential first-time homebuyers found that younger people put owning a home above financial security, getting fit, or even having children/starting a family. In 2019, the main reason for wanting to own a home was the fact that it provided a sense of security. Over a third of respondents also said that it was a means of future wealth preservation and that it was cheaper than renting".

These statistics highlight that this is a huge desire for many people, yet, I compare the analogy of the process to my own experience of climbing Mount Sinai in Egypt. Now, some may think this climb would be relatively easy, as it takes around four hours to complete, but, as this was my first experience of climbing any mountain, initially, it was challenging. This is how it may seem at the beginning of the process where you are not sure where to start, and before you have even started, what you are trying to achieve, can seem like an overwhelming challenge.

Before I started to ascend the mountain, I had to be prepared, taking into consideration any rules to follow. It is the same for the process when buying a property. You need to prepare for specific things in relation to finances, information, and certain personal records before you start to proceed. I will discuss this later on in the book.

In addition to this, I needed to be adequately equipped for the trek, which meant having the correct footwear, walking aids, and fluids. It is also key to be fully equipped for the purchase of buying a property; from having the correct people to support you, guide you, and provide you with knowledge through what can at times, seem like a minefield with many different people involved and lots of unfamiliar jargon.

I followed paths that were already prepared by those more experienced, although the terrain was rocky and the paths themselves were far from straightforward. Everyone's circumstances are unique to them. However, there may be cases where your circumstances are similar to someone else who bought a property before you, and following that particular path that had been completed previously, may work for you with the right guidance, though it may not be the most straightforward path.

Certain parts of the ascent on the mountain were hard! I couldn't see the top but had to persevere. My legs ached; I had to catch my breath many times, and occasionally slipped on rocks. Whenever we came to the places where we could stop for a break, there were times I felt like I didn't want to start again. The process of buying a property can feel exactly like this. As you go through the process, it may seem like there is still a lot to be done before you reach your end goal, and there can be a huge amount of paperwork involved. During these times, it may seem like you are moving forwards, but then suddenly, there is a delay or a slip-up that pulls you back. When these things happened, I had to focus on the end goal and keep going.

Starting the ascent and finishing the climb were the hardest parts. Once started, it was about getting used to the terrain, picking up a pace that worked for me, and trying to maintain the momentum. Then, as I got closer to the top, it got to a point where I wanted to get there, despite having a little way to go. Starting can be hard, and in the beginning stages, you may want to establish a certain pace in which you would like the purchase to proceed, and may take certain actions to create this pace to maintain momentum. As delays may occur during the process, even though you are getting towards the end, you may reach a point where you just want to see the end goal. It will sometimes take that little extra effort to get there.

The Property Process

Reaching the top of Mount Sinai was a most unforgettable experience. I remember feeling the bitterly cold air after starting in the early hours of the morning and ascending through the heat, to then seeing an amber glow across the wilderness of the desert and mountains as the sun began to rise. Being able to see the sunrise from the top after a difficult journey was such a beautiful moment. Although the process of buying a property may be difficult at times, reaching your end goal, receiving those keys in your hand, and knowing you are now officially a homeowner is the best feeling and makes the process seem worthwhile!

My aim for this book is to not only break down the process, but enable those who wish to proceed to buy their own property, to understand the process, and go through it with confidence and the ability to make informed decisions. My goal is that this book will also encourage you, through my own experiences and those of others that I share throughout sections of the book.

So, let's start this journey…

Chapter 1- Why buy?

For most people, this may seem like an obvious question: *Why do I want to buy a property?* However, it's a very important question to ask. This will help dictate what you are looking for, in terms of the types of property and area, keep you focused on your main priorities, and not get distracted. I will go into further detail about the things to consider when thinking about buying a property, but firstly, I want to look at some of the reasons for renting a property against buying a property.

Rent vs Buy

Although this book does focus on the buying process, it is important to consider whether renting or buying a property is more important to you, and some of the different reasons to think about, which is outlined in Table 1 below:

Table 1

RENTING	PURCHASE A PROPERTY
Easier to move home	Own the property
Lower maintenance costs (Landlord is responsible)	Autonomy (no Landlord)
Easier to budget	Use the equity in your home
Rent a bigger home in a desirable area	May be cheaper than renting

The Property Process

Firstly, renting can be a better option for some people. For example, a person may have a job that requires them to move frequently and stay in different places for several months at a time. For someone in this situation, buying a property may not be a suitable option they are willing to consider, as renting allows the freedom of movement to different properties, as and when the need arises.

Maintaining a property can be costly, especially when there are issues such as damp, windows needing replacement, or even if a new boiler needs to be installed. However, if you are renting, these costs will be the responsibility of the landlord, as long as they were not damaged by the tenant, and come under the terms and conditions of the tenancy agreement. Therefore, the lower maintenance costs for looking after the rented property is a cheaper and better option that also makes budgeting easier for some people.

Individuals may have various reasons for wanting to live in a bigger property and desirable area. If they were to buy, this could be a very expensive option for them. Therefore, renting may be a more suitable option that may allow them to achieve this.

Now, let us look at some of the reasons why people may choose to buy a property. It may be the case that, mortgage repayments are cheaper than rent, so in the long term, the buyer saves more money. Another more obvious reason is that buying allows the person to own the property, either if bought outright or once the mortgage is paid off. For many buyers, it provides them with more security, knowing they will eventually own their home and are not dealing with various occurrences that can happen when renting. For example, a landlord may decide to sell their property and, therefore, the tenant will need to seek alternative accommodation, or as another example, there may be an increase in the tenant's rental payments at some point.

Buying also allows people to utilise equity – this is the difference between the *value* of a property and the *amount* of mortgage outstanding on the property. Throughout the years, property prices can fluctuate. In the case where the property has increased in value over a period of time, homeowners may have the opportunity to release some, or all of the equity from the home. Professional advice needs to be sought for this.

However, it can be of great benefit as it allows the buyer to make future purchases, use the money for home improvements, or buy a bigger property, for example.

One final reason that someone may want to buy a property is to have more **autonomy**. When renting a property, if you wish to make small or significant changes, such as painting the walls a particular colour, the tenancy agreement may have restrictions, which state that you need to seek permission from the landlord. However, if you buy and own the property, you can decorate and rearrange the layout according to your needs and taste, without seeking further permission, unless there are certain restrictions due to the property being a listed building, or if planning permission is required for example.

Taking the time to consider some of these advantages and disadvantages can be a very valuable activity, as it helps to evaluate whether buying your first property is something you want to proceed with. Once this has been considered, the next step is to look in detail at reasons you want to buy your first property.

Commuting

Due to the location of workplaces, or the nature of someone's job role, they may need to commute. This could, therefore, be a real driving factor for someone wanting to purchase a property. Depending on the area in which the property is situated, it may make their commuting time a lot shorter, or sometimes longer, but with a scenic view, depending on what that person wants.

Family

Do you want to be closer to relatives? Has your family grown, or do you intend to start a family? All of these questions require consideration, as they will be key in deciding your area and type of property, which I will talk about later in the book.

The Property Process

Schools

Schools can be another key factor for wanting to buy. Getting a place in a school that the parent / child likes can be challenging sometimes for many reasons, therefore, some buyers may want to move into catchment areas, so that they have a better chance of accessing those schools. Alternatively, if you are looking to start a family, buying near schools is also something to consider for the future.

Change of Circumstances

For some people, the desire to buy a property could be due to a change of circumstances. This could be a better job which has increased their income, having a new partner, or sadly when a relative has passed away and the individual(s) may receive an inheritance as a result. Could this be one of the reasons why you want to buy now? Before you start looking, ask yourself the following questions:

1) "Is buying right for me and my goals?"

2) "What are the key reasons for me wanting to buy?"

It is important to be clear on this and it will help you stay focused during the process.

Chapter 2 - Your Team

Before going into further detail about finding the right property, area, and doing due diligence, the next step of the process should be to seek the right team to support you through this process.

Andrew Carnegie says: *"Teamwork is the ability to work together toward a common vision. The ability to direct individual accomplishments toward organizational objectives. It is the fuel that allows common people to attain uncommon results." – (1000 brilliant achievement quotes: Advice from the world's wisest, David Deford).*

This is a key part of the process, as they will be of such value moving forward in your purchase process, and ensuring they are there to support you. They are professionals who will provide guidance, support, advice, and ideas for buyers. If chosen correctly, they can really contribute to a smoother purchase process, as well as developing a long-term relationship with trustworthy professionals, who will keep your best interests at the forefront of the support they provide.

I have used the same team for a number of years because each one of them are knowledgeable and still willing to learn in their specialist areas. They are also solution finders. Wherever there are issues, I know they will always work with me to find a suitable solution. My team are landlords themselves, so when I was buying investments, they understood and tailored their advice specifically for this, while sharing their own experiences. At the time of writing this book, we were going through the Coronavirus Pandemic, and because of this, I constantly kept in regular contact to ensure I am aware of changes in the market and updates in legislation while being able to discuss different options with them. So, who are the key members of your team when buying a property?

Mortgage Advisor

The role of a mortgage advisor is to advise you on the best mortgage for your goals and personal circumstances. Mortgage advisors may also provide extra services on relevant insurances and protection if they are qualified to do so. To seek the right mortgage, they will normally ask for personal information such as your income, which can be from payslips you receive from your job, as well as any benefits, you may receive, for example. They will also require information such as any debts including credit cards or loans, and any other financial commitments such as overdrafts, if you have bought something on finance, such as a car, and if you have children or additional store cards.

They may also ask for your credit file, which is a credit report that outlines your credit history i.e. any cards you own, any debts you have, the frequency of payments that have been made on time, and any defaults - payments not made on time, County Court Judgements (CCJ) and other useful information. I personally like to use a website called **https://www.checkmyfile.com/**. However, there are many other websites you can use.

A story I was told really opened my eyes and helped me to understand what some lenders look for in credit files. Credit reports generate a number based on whether you have good credit or bad credit. Someone that has a high score of 999 may think they have a perfect credit score, but unless you look at the details, this may not be the case. Someone who has a perfect score of 999, may still have difficulty in accessing lending for a mortgage. When looking into the detail of this credit report, they had a number of payday loans.

What this meant was, on the report, the payday loan was being paid off at the right time, and therefore, the score was high. However, many lenders viewed the payday loan as a risk, because the individual may have taken it due to financial difficulties, and therefore, some mortgage lenders were not willing to lend. In comparison, there is someone whose credit score is fair; however because of their financial behaviour i.e. making credit card payments on time, they were able to secure a mortgage.

Subsequently, it is good to keep a regular check on your credit report and seek advice before taking certain actions that may result in affecting your credit report. By doing this, where possible, you can monitor changes in the *detail* of your credit report. I should also say that every individual's financial situation is different and that the above examples were scenarios used to explain and understand what lenders may look for. However, whatever your financial situation is, it is good to have an open discussion about it to see if there are any options for you, as well as getting a good understanding of what you can do to improve your credit file, if necessary.

There are various types of mortgage advisors. Some may be restricted, and therefore, linked to a specific lender within a bank for example. Rather than having access to a number of different lenders, they will only be able to talk about the mortgage products within that particular bank, and this may or may not work for you and your circumstances. There are also *independent mortgage advisors* who have access to a wider range of different lenders, which is useful, as they may be able to provide a good rate for you. It is also important to ensure you discuss why you are buying and what your future plans are.

This may seem like a lot of information to provide; however, it allows the mortgage advisor to get a holistic understanding of your current circumstances. This helps them to ensure they look for a lender who will work for your current circumstances, allow you to purchase the type of property you desire, and utilise the property in the way you wish, as well as taking into consideration your future plans.

This also allows the mortgage advisor to work out what is known as your affordability. This is a calculation that is done to estimate how much a lender is likely to offer you. Some say 4.5 times of your annual salary, but it's more complex, as other factors are also taken into consideration.

Keep in mind that this is only an estimate, and therefore, the final amount they are willing to lend may change once they have assessed all the information they request from the buyer. I will go into this in further detail, but this piece of information is really useful as a starting point and can be incorporated into your research on areas and types of properties you may want to look for.

When looking for a mortgage advisor, there are a range of things you can ask or do:

Ask for recommendations

Ask family and friends to provide recommendations. Estate agents may offer their mortgage advisor/mortgage broker, but please note, you are not obligated to use them because they are selling the property to you; it is always good to seek other alternatives.

Online Websites

Websites such as **https://www.unbiased.co.uk/** can be used to search for professional advisors. It is also worthwhile to check if they are authorised by the Financial Conduct Authority (FCA) which means they are authorised to advise you.

Ask Questions

When searching for mortgage advisors, ask questions such as:

- "Do you have access to the whole of the market?"

- "What are your fees?" – A mortgage advisor should inform you of how the payment fees should be made, once they have provided you with information on a suitable lender, and the interest rate. If you are happy to proceed, some may charge an upfront fee, whilst some may not charge anything, as they get a commission from the lender. Others may charge a percentage of the purchase price of the property.

- "Are you regulated?"

- "How will you keep me updated on my application?"

If you are unsure of anything, do not be afraid to ask questions. I remember asking many questions when purchasing my first property. I was eager to learn, understand, and make informed decisions during the process of my mortgage application. As my advisor always says, "No question is a silly question!"

Your mortgage advisor should also be proactive. As there are many types of mortgages, which I will discuss later in the book, it is important to be clear about your reasons for buying, the type of property you are buying, and your future plans.

Depending on what offers are available at the time, a mortgage advisor may recommend that a particular mortgage product which is suitable for your circumstances, will be offered to you on a 25-year period, but have a fixed rate of interest for five years. That means you will have a set interest rate, and therefore, a set monthly amount to pay for five years.

Although it has been offered for a 25-year period, a few months before the five years of fixed interest payments are due to expire, the mortgage advisor may get in touch to discuss whether it may be more cost-effective to move to another suitable mortgage product. This can be very useful to assess, especially if the mortgage payments drastically increase once the fixed term ends. This is an example of what I mean by having a proactive mortgage advisor and is key for managing monthly payments to achieve long term goals.

Overall, a good mortgage advisor will be essential to the purchasing of your property, so take the time to look around.

Summary:

- Ask key questions when looking for a mortgage advisor.

- Make sure they are regulated.

- Decide which type of mortgage advisor will be right for you.

- Provide information about your current financial situation, or type of property you like, and future plans.

The Property Process

Estate Agents

Generally speaking, most people who wish to sell their property will instruct an estate agent to help them. As a buyer, an estate agent is another key member of your team to help in finding a property to suit your needs. As they are in the business of selling properties, they have access to a wide range of properties. It is also a good idea to check if they are a member of a professional body, such as **NAEA Propertymark**. When looking for estate agents, it is likely you will come across four types including:

1) National Chains

National chain estate agents have offices across the country, which normally have glass frontages with a number of staff at desks where you can pop-in to have a chat, and they may have a large selection of properties.

2) Independent Agents

Independent estate agents are much smaller, in comparison to national chains and operate within a smaller radius locally. Generally speaking, they have a smaller number of properties to sell.

3) Online Estate Agents

Online estate agents do not have a physical office where you can visit; however, they are accessible for longer periods and can attend to you at any time e.g. online web chats.

4) Hybrid Estate Agents

Hybrid estate agents are based online and provide services that a national chain or independent agent may offer, such as allocating a local expert for viewings.

The Property Process

When searching for a property, it is a good idea to view properties that are of interest to you, with several different agents to get a feel of which one will work best for your needs. Estate agents can also be very knowledgeable about the area in which you want to buy. Keeping in regular contact builds rapport and a good understanding of what you are looking for.

A good estate agent will also work to push your offer through if you are able to put forward good reasons for the offer you have made. These can include having the proof of deposit available or not being involved in a chain - which is where more than one transaction takes place so that the purchase and sale of properties of those involved in the chain can be completed.

When I bought my first property, I worked with a small independent agent that understood what I was looking for, and was always able to arrange viewings for properties that were of interest to me. When it came to putting forward an offer on a property of interest, the seller had to decide between another buyer and me.

The estate agent encouraged the seller to proceed with my offer, even though it was similar to the offer made by the other buyer, which I later found out. This was agreed nonetheless, as the seller wanted a quick sale, I was in a position to proceed quickly. Keep in mind that the other role of the estate agent is to achieve the best possible price for their client and may attempt to push up your offer. I will talk about this in more detail later in the book.

They may also have in-house services such as mortgage brokers and solicitors that they may encourage you to use. It is important to know that you are not, in any way, obliged to do so and this should not affect the sale if you do not use them. Look around so that you can compare quotes and services. As with all the other members of your team, you also need to ensure that you communicate the following:

- What your specific needs are.

- Give them a brief of what you are looking for including the number of bedrooms, off-road parking and a garden, for example.

- Make them aware of your position. If you are a first-time buyer for example, inform them of this.

- Give them a rough idea of your budget if they ask.

Although it may seem like estate agents can have a conflicting role, as they are working on behalf of the seller, they should still be considered as a **key member** of your team that will support you in finding a suitable property.

<u>Summary</u>

- Inform estate agents about your brief.

- Contact different types of estate agents.

- Inform the agent of your position if you are a first-time buyer, for example.

- Check whether the agent is a member of a professional body such as NAEA Propertymark (National Association of Estate Agents).

Solicitors and Licensed Conveyancers

The next key person in your team will be your solicitor or licensed conveyancer. Their role is to guide and support you through the legal aspects of purchasing a property, ensuring that the property is purchased lawfully, and inform you of any issues that arise.

The difference between a *solicitor* and *licensed conveyancer* is stated below:

- A licenced conveyancer specialises in property transactions.

- A solicitor offers full additional legal services.

Some solicitors may be able to handle more complex purchases, but as a result, it may cost more to use their services, yet still be a better option for you.

They are also regulated by the Solicitors Regulation Authority (SRA) or the Council of Licensed Conveyancers (CLC) and are registered with the Law Society, so it is a good idea to check these online. Similar to the actions of a mortgage advisor when they first engage with the buyer, there is information the solicitor or licensed conveyancer will request from you to ensure they can progress with the legal aspects of the purchase and support you with any questions or negotiations with the seller. They may ask for the following:

- *Completed client questionnaire* – this includes information such as your name, current address, bank details, details of the mortgage lender, and details of the property you are purchasing.

- *Evidence* – of where the deposit fund has come from. This is to avoid unlawful activities like money laundering.

They will also provide:

- *Terms of business* - which outlines information such as their services, key people in their team, and how your data is used.

- *An outline of their costs and fees* – Some fees may be fixed, whilst others may be an estimate because there are variables during the transaction that can result in a change of the fees and costs. For example, if the purchase is in progress, and you as the buyer, decide to negotiate on the price because of an issue that has arisen, this will have an impact on the final fees and costs.

The Property Process

There are key questions to ask a solicitor or licensed conveyancer before making a final decision to instruct them. These include:

- "What are your costs?" – ensure this is itemised and if there are timeframes for specific payments.

- "Are you approved by my mortgage lender?"

- "How will you keep me updated and how often?"

- "Who will manage my case?"

- "Do you have previous experience of dealing with a case similar to mine?"

- "Which professional bodies are you members of?"

- "What are your office opening hours, and will you be closed on any other day outside of this in the near future?"

It is also useful to look up reviews online and see if they have been recommended by others. Find out about the individual/client's experience of using them. It is important to note that you are not obliged to use the estate agents' solicitors. Be sure to look around and compare costs.

If you are buying a property, your solicitor or licensed conveyancer will inform the seller's solicitors that they have been instructed by you, and request a draft contract. Your solicitor or licenced conveyancer will carry out the legal searches, which provides specific information about the property that you may not be aware of. Certain information may also be required by the mortgage lender.

The searches can include the following:

- ***Checking the Title Deeds*** – This is a document on Land Registry that confirms the legal ownership of the property.

- *Water Searches* – This helps to find out where your water supply comes from and where drains are situated.

- *Environmental Search* – This provides information about whether the property is near or on contaminated land and if your property is in a flood-risk area.

- *Local Authority Search* – this provides information about any upcoming developments near your property. For example, if a wind turbine farm is going to be built, or a new motorway.

- *Chancel Liability Search* – this informs you if you are liable for the maintenance costs of local churches, which was something that was put in place in medieval times.

- *Conditions* – they will look at the conditions within your mortgage offer.

- *Contract Examination* – they will examine the contract. It is also your responsibility to go through it to ensure you are happy that any queries have been dealt with, and all the expected fixtures and fittings in the property are agreed and a suitable completion date has been agreed.

- *Buildings Insurance* – If applicable, they will ask you to have buildings insurance in place before exchanging contracts. Once the contract is signed, they will exchange the contracts, transfer your name(s) on to the title deeds and register at Land Registry.

Ensure that you ask your solicitor about any paperwork if you are not certain. Many of the documents contain legal terminology, and therefore, having a discussion with the solicitor over the phone or email can be helpful in understanding what certain documents mean. Make sure your solicitor is *proactive*. I have personally experienced the difference between a proactive and non-proactive solicitor.

For example, if the solicitor is not being proactive, it can have a knock-on-effect on delaying the process. Therefore, if the mortgage offer is valid for a certain number of months, but the delay results in exceeding this timeframe, this may cause the mortgage offer to expire. Consequently, the buyer may have to ask if they can extend the timeframe of the mortgage offer, or start the mortgage application again.

Additionally, if they are not proactive, and you are purchasing during a particular time of the year, such as Easter or Christmas where offices may be closed, you may have to contact them more frequently to ensure you push forward the process. In comparison, if you have a proactive solicitor, you will find that they will contact you regularly to keep you updated with the process, and will answer any questions promptly, informing you of any issues that arise in the searches and advise accordingly.

Although some purchases may not be straightforward with any solicitor or licensed conveyancer, having a professional that is proactive and supportive makes the purchase less stressful, compared to those that are not. Whether you do decide to use a solicitor or licensed conveyancer, they should be a key member of your team who works on your behalf to help you understand what you are buying, and provide support in proceeding with your transaction.

Summary

- Think about your purchase and whether you want to use a solicitor or licensed conveyancer.

- Ask key questions when searching around for a solicitor.

- Ensure they are members of a professional body.

- Ensure regular communication is maintained.

- Ask questions if you are unsure about certain documents and ensure that any enquiries are dealt with promptly.

Mortgage Lender

For many buyers, this is the route that is often utilised when you don't have the cash to buy a property outright. Once you provide a certain percentage of the deposit, which is your own money that is put towards buying a property, following a successful application, the mortgage lender will loan you the outstanding amount for the purchase. The amount loaned is secured against the property.

Whether an application is successful or not, is decided by the mortgage underwriter, who is employed by the mortgage lender to assess the applicant. There are some mortgage lenders who can only be accessed via a mortgage advisor and others where individuals can access directly.

There are certain documents such as passports, bank statements, payslips, and utility bills as proof of address that lenders use to verify your identity and carry out assessments on your financial behaviours. The information mortgage lenders request will depend on which lender you use and the complexity of your purchase.

Surveyor

A surveyor is someone who does a complete inspection of a property and checks the condition of various aspects of the property. If the buyer is taking a mortgage, it can be useful to look for a suitable surveyor once they have received their confirmed mortgage offer.

When buying a property, some buyers do not want to use a surveyor for many reasons, including keeping the costs down. You are not obliged to do so as part of the purchase, however, I have found them to be quite useful, as they provided information that contributed to my understanding of whether this was the type of property I would be interested in buying. The price of surveys differs, depending on the type of survey carried out and the property that is being purchased. When I bought my first property, I made the mistake of assuming the mortgage valuation was the same as having a detailed survey completed.

The Property Process

A mortgage valuation is normally carried out as a requirement for the mortgage lender, and the buyer may or may not have to pay for this, depending on the lender they use.

This type of valuation outlines whether the property you desire to buy is worth the amount you have agreed to pay. This enables the mortgage lender to check whether the loan will be covered in the event that they have to repossess the property. Mortgage valuations can be carried out in different ways. Some may be done online, where they analyse sales data in the area. They may also drive by the property, while others may require physically viewing the property.

If a buyer decides to use a surveyor, the surveyor should ideally be a member of the Royal Institution of Chartered Surveyors (RICS), and offer at least three different types of surveys:

- ***Condition Report*** – A condition report is a basic survey that provides a summary of potential risks and problems in the property. This type of survey does not include any further advice or a valuation of the property.

- ***Homebuyers Report*** – A homebuyer's report provides a more detailed report of the internal and external condition of the property, outlining any issues, recommendations, and photographs. Some homebuyer reports can also include a valuation at an additional cost.

- ***Buildings Survey*** – The building survey is the most in-depth survey that a surveyor will carry out. This will involve aspects such as looking in attics. The comprehensive report will include recommendations for repairs and the estimated time it may take to be completed, as well as estimated costs for the repairs. The report will also include photos and outline what could happen, should the recommended repairs not be carried out, though it does not usually include a valuation of the property.

Properties that need full refurbishment and are in poor condition may benefit from a buildings survey carried out by a local surveyor. However, others who are buying a property in reasonable condition may choose to have a homebuyer's report carried out.

The decision as to whether you have a survey completed and which type of survey you choose is entirely your decision. It's good to take into consideration the type of property you want to buy, knowing its condition. I have found surveys very helpful as they highlight issues that I wouldn't have known just by looking at the property.

As a result of the estimated costs of repairs outlined in the report, I had been able to re-negotiate on the price of the property, or the seller has offered to carry out the repair, before completing and exchanging on the property. A more recent issue that is now being highlighted is cladding on flats and surveyors can help with highlighting potential issues, though your solicitor or licenced conveyancer will need to seek further reports.

If you are buying a new build property, it is also a good idea to mention this to the surveyor, as they may provide a snagging survey to suit. Surveys are an additional cost and there is the risk of losing the money if the sale falls through. However, as I mentioned before, buying a property is a big financial commitment, so you may want to consider paying for a survey, rather than buying a property with potential unwanted surprises!

Summary

- Look for local surveyors as they are likely to know the area well.

- Check if your surveyor is a member of RICS.

- Speak to a few surveyors and decide which survey will be suitable for the type of property you are interested in.

Tradespeople

Tradespeople will only be relevant if the property you wish to buy requires refurbishment. They will be crucial in bringing your vision to reality within a timely and cost-effective manner.

If you also decide to manage the project yourself, keeping an eye on their quality of work, the progress, and your budget are all important. Finding a good tradesperson can be tricky. On an occasion, I drove for over an hour to attend a breakfast networking meeting at 6.00 am, trying to find a suitable tradesperson, before having to go to work later that day!

There are various websites where tradespeople advertise their services, online apps that can seek local tradespeople, and word of mouth which can be a great alternative method. Ask for recommendations from friends, family, and neighbours. They will be able to tell you their experiences of using a particular tradesperson. The person who has recommended their services may also be more than happy to show you around their home, so you have the opportunity to look at the quality of the work carried out.

Another great place to ask is estate agents. If they also have a lettings branch, as they manage a number of properties, it is likely that they will have regular contact with local tradespeople they use for the properties managed, and can, therefore, make recommendations. Also, go online and do an internet search on the company you are interested in working with. Do your own research and don't just take a person's word for it. If you need to use a tradesperson as part of your team, the following key steps are important for you to take:

Get Quotes

Before deciding on which tradesperson, you want to go with, ensure you get at least *three* quotes.

Ask the tradesperson whether they are willing to view the property you are interested in buying, so they can look around and make their own recommendations and assessments. If you decide to use a project manager to oversee all the works, they may charge for their time to view properties with you. Therefore it may be a good idea to arrange this once you have identified the property you are interested in.

Alternatively, when your offer has been accepted, you can arrange another viewing with them. Bear in mind that the quote they provide for the works should be not considered in isolation, but rather, as part of other factors such as whether the tradesperson has been recommended. It may be that you decide to use a tradesperson that didn't provide the cheapest quote, because, in comparison to other trades, they clearly outlined their costs and were recommended, due to their quality of work.

Get it in Writing

I have experienced tradespeople who have looked around properties with me and said verbally it will cost "x" amount to do this and "Don't worry about those little jobs! I will do them for nothing!". Be **very wary** of what is promised **verbally** as you have nothing to refer to, if the works discussed are not all completed, or costs spiral out of control. Get **all quotes** in writing. Ideally, it should be sent via email or post.

Get it Itemised

Some tradespeople do not like to itemise their costs, however, some will. Having itemised cost details is useful in understanding the difference between the cost of materials for the work, and the cost of their labour. It also gives you an overview of what materials will be provided for the project, and therefore, you can raise any queries around what has been outlined.

Is it an Estimate?

Due to the nature of some works that are carried out, such as installing new heating systems, until they start the work, they don't know if other issues may crop up, and therefore, may give you an estimate of the works. It is always useful to confirm whether the quote provided is an estimate to enable you to factor in unexpected added costs. Alternatively, the quote may be a final agreed cost, but again, it's always good to have a contingency budget in case things don't go to plan.

The Property Process

Does it include VAT?

Depending on what works are being carried out on your property, adding VAT can significantly change the final cost, so ask whether the quote includes VAT.

Ask to see any of their recent work and relevant insurance

It's a great idea to see any previous work they have completed, to see the standard of work and what you would expect should you use them. Also ask to see their public liability insurance cover as this may cover things such as, damage to your property or a neighbour's property, and someone being injured during refurbishment works to the property.

Ask Early!

A good tradesperson may not always be available to carry out the works immediately, because they are in high demand, and are likely to be working on other projects. Get in touch with a tradesperson early enough and ask them when they will be available. Find out if they are currently working on other projects and whether they are planning to be away at any point, as this may delay the project before it has even started!

Get the right trade in at the right time

If you are using a number of different tradespeople, make sure they can work around each other and get the right people in at the right time. For example, if the property needs a full refurbishment, the tradespeople will normally come in the following order:

- **Plumbing** - As pipework needs to run through the floors and walls, they will be one of the first trades.

- **Electrics** - As the wiring feeds through the floors and walls, they will need to come early.

- **External Doors and Windows** - Walls and flooring may be damaged, and would need to be fixed on time.

- **Plastering** – The next step is to work on damaging walls and floors by filling the holes and making the walls smooth.

- **Fittings** – This consists of the installation of things such as the bathroom, kitchen, and fitted wardrobes.

- **Woodwork** – This includes fittings such as spindles in staircases, skirting, and architraves.

- **Painting** - This should happen towards the end of the work finally being completed. The necessary walls and other areas are in conditions that can be painted. As it can be messy, it will not damage the flooring, as this will be laid at a later stage.

- **Final Electric Fit** – Such as sockets and switches.

- **Flooring** - Depending on the type of flooring you decide to choose, whether it is carpet with underlay, vinyl with plywood underneath, or tiles, doing the flooring at this stage minimises any potential damage from other previous aspects of the refurbishment. Though in some circumstances skirting boards may be fitted after the flooring is laid.

- **Internal Doors** - This is helpful so that all the doors in the property will be accurate, and won't have issues with the bottom of the door scraping along a brand-new carpet, for example, due to the change in the height of the flooring once the carpet was initially laid.

If you don't understand, ASK!

Tradespeople, depending on what they do, will be very knowledgeable in their specialist areas. They may talk about certain materials or techniques that the buyer may not have heard of.

I remember speaking to various tradespeople and they were referring to words such as flue, BTU, coving or acclimatising flooring, and receiving a blank expression from me, as I had no idea about what any of those words meant!

It was important for me to ask at the beginning to learn more about what they do, and understand why or how it will be used. Doing a refurbishment requires paying for materials and the tradesperson's labour and expertise, so if you are unsure about anything, ask, because some tradespeople may assume that you know what they are talking about.

Communicate with the tradesperson if something doesn't look right, or you feel it won't work. For example, a friend of mine who bought her first property was carrying out refurbishments and needed a small radiator to be placed under one of the windows. When she saw what the tradesperson ordered online, the size did not look right.

Instead of leaving it, she asked the plumber to check, which he did. Had the plumber installed it, it wouldn't have fitted in that particular space. Make sure the tradesperson double-checks what they have ordered, as they also can make mistakes.

Factor in the Additional Costs

When purchasing a property that needs refurbishment, depending on its state, it may be that the new homeowner will not be able to move in straight away. If this is the case and the buyer decides to remain in their current rental property, while the works are being carried out, one of the factors to consider is the additional costs of paying for two properties. This includes twice the council tax, electricity, and gas, as well as the rent where they currently live, and mortgage payments on their new property.

This requires consideration as depending on the individual's financial circumstances, it may or may not be feasible to cover these costs over a long period of time. Other issues may come to light during refurbishment and can cause further delays. The new homeowner will need to decide whether they wish to rectify these issues and pay the cost attached, as well as potentially paying for the two properties over a longer period, because of the unexpected delays.

To save on additional costs with this type of purchase, the buyer may consider the option of moving in with relatives or friends, while the works are being carried out to potentially save money.

Arrange to make Payment at Different Stages

I've heard a few sad stories of some tradespeople who took money from homeowners and did not complete the job, which resulted in the homeowner losing a lot of money. For the very few tradespeople that do this, it can be devastating for the homeowner.

To try and alleviate the risk of this happening, it is best to make payments at different stages of the refurbishment, and not make the full payment upfront. If the tradesperson is doing the whole refurbishment with a team of other specialists, the homeowner may decide to make three payments over an agreed timeframe. The first payment at an agreed time, once the works have started, the second payment partway through the refurbishment, and finally, the last payment once the work has been completed, checked thoroughly, and any snags rectified.

Alternatively, if it is a smaller job such as installing a new back door, the homeowner may decide to make a small payment at the beginning, and complete the final payment towards the end, once they have checked over the works and are happy with the finished look. Make sure you discuss this with your tradesperson, prior to the works commencing. Get the agreed timeframe and payments *in writing*, and check that you are happy with the works that are carried out at each stage, highlighting any issues before making a payment.

Finding a good, reliable tradesperson can save time and money in the long run, and all the factors should contribute to providing a holistic picture of a particular tradesperson. This will influence your decision on the person you hire, but moreover, grant more control over making an informed choice.

The Operational Process

The diagram below is a simple breakdown of the buying process and outlines at what stage of the process each member of the team will be working with the buyer:

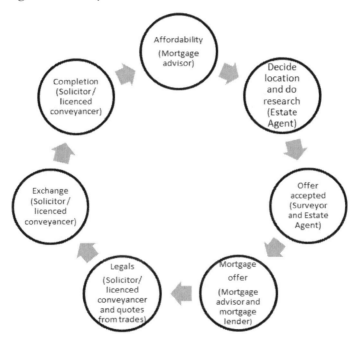

The estate agent or seller will normally request updates. It is good practice for the buyer to keep track of the progress, therefore, it is important to maintain regular communication with all the parties. Now you know the role of each person in your team; the next step is to look at how you are going to buy the property.

Chapter 3 - Finance

Finance is a big consideration and will be for most people when buying a home. It is one of the greatest factors, and something I would always advise to get professional guidance on before looking at the options of purchasing a property, as everyone's circumstances are different. I will share my experiences and those of others outlining how we raised finances and purchased our first properties, however, keep in mind that each experience is tailored for an individual's circumstance and future plans at the time, and therefore, what may have been a good action to take for one, may not work for another:

Savings

Savings is something that I learnt to do from a young age, although it frequently had its ups and downs! From the age of 16 when I worked in various retail jobs earning £6.75 an hour, once I received my monthly pay, I set up a direct debit to go into my savings account, and 10% of the rest of my wages to go into my ISA savings account. At the time, this was not much, however, in three years, it totalled £1,404. Doing this, in addition to my wage increase enabled me to have a pot of over £6,000 to utilise. This showed how doing this regularly can compound over a number of years. There is a great book by Darren Hardy called **The Compound Effect** that explains this in detail and is worth reading.

At the time, I was not saving for anything specific, but it helped to put towards the deposit for my purchase. Once I was getting educated on how to invest in property, I also looked at other ways of saving towards a deposit. I made a very conscious decision to cut down on non-essential spending, such as buying lunch, going out with friends regularly for dinner, and buying clothes or accessories.

Things like breakfast that I loved to buy on my way to work cost £4.00 that I bought at least three times a week. When I cut it down, it enabled me to save £48.00 a month. I started selling unwanted gifts and unworn clothes on eBay and money I received would range from £5.00 up to £300.00, depending on what I was selling and how often I did this. I also cancelled subscriptions I didn't need and continued to live at home with my mum so I didn't have to pay large amounts of rent.

Nowadays, there are various money-saving challenges and apps that can be found through doing internet searches, which make it more of a fun task to do. There are other steps that have been taken to raise finances in more creative ways which I will outline below, but before taking action on any of these steps, a big lesson I learnt is to get professional advice on your exit strategies.

What this means, essentially, is having a plan ahead of time on how to pay back any additional borrowing and working out figures on a worst-case scenario. This helps towards making sure the numbers would still work or be manageable, before taking on any potential debt, so that it lessens the risk of putting the borrower and potentially others in difficult financial situations, which could have negative long term effects. With this in mind, here are some of the other steps:

Asking Others

Asking friends and relatives was something I was very uncomfortable with, initially, as I am the type of person that does not like asking people for financial help. However, the way I overcame this was by telling myself that the money was going toward a long-term investment for the future. I would ensure we agreed on a plan, which was put in place to pay them back, discuss any potential issues, and assess the worst-case scenario. The worst that could happen is hearing them say no and if I didn't ask for help, it would take much longer to get to a point where I had enough money to buy a property.

As a result of asking others, I had different reactions. Some said no because they didn't have the means to help. Others said they would think about it, whilst I received a few yes's! I only felt able to do this with close family and friends, and as a result, I was able to raise additional funds towards the costs of the purchase, such as the fees and deposit, some of which were paid back over an agreed period of time. Some of the people that agreed to help out surprised me, and granted me the money as a gift; therefore, they did not expect me to pay back. Others that I did not expect to say yes said the money was not doing anything so they were happy to support.

Loans, Credit Cards, and Switching Accounts

I remember asking my mortgage advisor if I could take out a loan to use towards the deposit. She went on to explain that I can't **borrow to borrow** because a loan is borrowed money that I had to pay back. I can't use the borrowed money to request more lending in the form of a mortgage. A big part of this was that mortgage lending had to be assessed properly to ensure that I could afford payments based on factors such as my income and how much debt I had at the time.

In addition to our discussion about loans, we looked at how to use credit cards responsibly. We also spoke about an alternative option; if I didn't have the full funds upfront for the refurbishment, I could consider the option of transferring money from a credit card via a money transfer. This would solely be used towards the refurbishment of the property. Some credit cards offered 0% interest on money transfers, which is essentially transferring cash from a credit card to a debit card which, in this particular scenario, would only be used towards the refurbishments.

My advisor would not recommend obtaining a large amount of credit to finance a refurbishment. We also had to get calculations of the purchase right from the beginning and explore other exit strategies if things didn't go to plan. We also discussed current credit card debt, and how to manage it by paying more than the minimum monthly payments.

If there was an outstanding amount on the credit card as a result of the money transfer and the 0% interest period was due to expire, we discussed transferring the balance on to a different credit card. This would be done via a 0% interest balance transfer for a specific period so that interest is not paid on the balance of the credit card. Also ensuring regular overpayments per month are being made to clear the balance.

We spoke about the risks if this route was not used responsibly. This included potentially having unmanageable payments if interest was added due to the 0% period ending, which would then take longer to pay off. I could also accumulate more debt and my credit file could also be negatively affected if I missed payments.

Another route that was considered was seeking bank accounts that offered cash incentives for switching to their bank if I met the criteria. Again, before using this route, the implications on my credit file of opening another bank account was also considered and discussed. Finding ways of raising finances can seem overwhelming, not only in putting down a deposit, but also the additional costs, such as the cost of a surveyor, legal conveyancing fees and stamp duty when buying a property.

However, everyone's personal circumstances and financial situations aren't the same. Each option has its own advantages and disadvantages, so it is important to seek advice from a qualified professional before taking any steps to decide which route will work in favour of your current circumstances and future plans. With this in mind, here are some other suggestions that you may want to explore:

Downsize

I know of people who were renting and made the decision to look at ways of lowering their rental payments in order to save for their first home. Some decided to rent a smaller property; others decided to rent a room, while others decided to move back with their parents. These options allowed them to save much more which was used towards buying their home.

Become a Property Guardian

Another option could be to become a property guardian. This is where people can live in safe buildings for a low rental payment, normally under a licence to occupy agreement. This helps safeguard and secure the building whilst it is empty. You can get more information from websites such as **www.adhocproperty.co.uk** and **www.dotdotdotproperty.com** to see their criteria and more information.

Use a Scheme

There are many schemes available, which are always changing, due to government alterations. Below is further information about a few schemes that are currently available (at the time of writing this) and how they work. Professional advice should be sought to discuss the eligibility criteria, and whether it is suitable for your current circumstances and future plans.

Help-to-Buy Equity Loan Scheme

The Help-to-Buy Equity Loan scheme is where the government provides an equity loan to buy newly built homes. First-time buyers and existing homeowners are eligible, subject to certain criteria being met. You can get more information from the **https://www.helptobuy.gov.uk/** and find your nearest help to buy agent. The purchase price of the property must be no more than £600,000 and you can borrow 20% of the purchase price, interest-free, for the first five years, as long as you have at least a 5% deposit. If you are purchasing in London, you can borrow 40% of the purchase price.

The scheme has been extended from 2021 to 2023 and after April 2021 it will only be offered to first-time buyers, and include property price caps. The loan must be paid at the end of your mortgage term, or if you sell your home, whichever happens first. You can also pay back some or your entire equity loan without selling your home. However, you must pay the same percentage of the proceeds of the sale, plus the initial equity loan.

The Property Process

Here is an example:

Purchase price - £200,000.

This will consist of the following:

Your deposit 5% - £10,000.

Equity loan 20% - £40,000.

Mortgage 75% - £150,000.

If you then decide to sell, and the property is now worth £250,000, there is an increase in the value of 25% (£50,000), so you would pay:

- ***The Equity Loan Repayment*** – (The original loan of £40,000 + 25% profit which equates to £10,000. This is because was a 25% increase in value and therefore this must also be paid on the amount borrowed).

- ***Mortgage*** – £150,000 (less the capital repayments - this is the monthly repayments that contribute towards paying down the mortgage, excluding any interest). You are left with at least £50,000 or more, depending on how much is left on your mortgage. This can be used as a deposit on your next home. After the first five years of the interest-free period, in year six, you pay interest of 1.75% in addition to the loan.

From year seven onwards, 1.75%, plus the retail prices index (RPI) inflation measures, plus an additional 1%.

<u>Example</u>

- From year seven, if the RPI is 3%, the interest rate would rise to 4% (3% + the additional 1%).
- 4% of the original 1.75% interest is 0.07%.

- 0.07% will be added to the original 1.75% and therefore, the rate will rise to 1.82%

- The loan must be paid off either once the property is sold, the mortgage is paid off, or the equity loan term has ended.

<u>Right to Acquire</u>

You can be eligible for the Right to Acquire scheme if you've had a public sector landlord for three years and lived in a housing association property built after 1997 or transferred to a housing association property after 1997. You are able to buy your property at a discount if you live in a property owned by a housing association. The maximum discount is £16,000 and the discount depends on where you are buying (location).

If you sell within the first five years of ownership, the discount you initially received may have to be paid back. In addition to this, the property must first be offered to your landlord within the first 10 years, and the scheme is no longer available in Wales and Scotland.

<u>Shared Ownership</u>

The Shared Ownership scheme is only for first-time buyers and non-homeowners, so you could have previously owned a property, but do not own one now, earn £80,000 or less and have enough savings to cover a 5% deposit of the share you are buying. You can buy between 25-75% share of the home which is normally new builds, or resale housing association homes. I have included an example below if you were to own a 25% share of the property and 75% is owned by the housing association:

The Property Process

Purchase price - £200,000.

Housing association share - £150,000 (75%).

Your share £50,000 (25%).

Your deposit £2,500 (5% of the value of your share).

Mortgage required £47,500.

With shared ownership, you pay the rent and the service charge on the share you don't own.

There are also some additional points you may want to consider with shared ownership:

- You have the opportunity to own a brand-new home that is likely to be energy efficient.

- You pay a lower deposit.

- Shared ownership properties can be leasehold properties sold by housing associations and private developers. Therefore, the shareowner is liable for additional maintenance costs and service charges.

- Some shared ownership buyers may want to increase the percentage of the amount they own of the property – this is known as *staircasing*. There can be restrictions to consider, such as the percentage, and the minimum of which you can own. Therefore, if you wish to own a higher percentage or eventually 100% of the property, it is a good idea to plan ahead, as the property price may rise. This may result in you having to put forward a larger amount to own that percentage.

- The developers may encourage you to use recommended mortgage advisors/mortgage brokers, solicitors, and other services, but you are not obliged to do so, as it is always a good idea to look elsewhere to compare different options. Using independent professionals should not affect your purchase.

- You may need to ask for permission to redecorate or change the structure of your home.

- If you decide to sell your home, certain restrictions and criteria may need to be met. In the first instance, the housing association or developer may also have the right to seek a new buyer within a certain timeframe, before you can put the property for sale on the open market.

- The housing association or private developer still owns the rental part of the property.

There are also two other types of Shared Ownership schemes:

1) *Home Ownership for People with Long-Term Disabilities (HOLD)* - If a person has a long-term disability and needs a property to meet their needs, they can apply for HOLD if the property is for sale under shared ownership.

2) *Older People's Shared Ownership* – This scheme allows people aged 55 and over to buy up to 75% of a property. Once they own a maximum of 75%, they no longer have to pay rent on the remaining share.

Rent to Buy

Rent to Buy in England, Northern Ireland and Scotland, is a government scheme which is also sometimes named, Rent Save Buy or Rent to Save. This scheme aims to help first-time buyers by giving eligible individual(s) the opportunity to rent a new build property at around 80% of the market rate for a maximum period of five years, therefore allowing the individual to save towards a deposit, though they are not obliged to do so.

The Property Process

Throughout this period, the individual(s) will have the opportunity to purchase the property fully, buy a share of the property using the Shared Ownership scheme or move. To be eligible for this scheme, individual(s) must be first-time buyers or previous homeowners who no longer can afford to purchase a property on the market, and who have a household income of £60,000 or less outside of London, and £64,300 in London.

- In addition to this, there is an added criterion that must be met for different housing associations.

- The individual(s) must hold a good credit report.

Unfortunately, there have been a very limited number of properties built under this scheme, so it can be tricky to utilise. Wales has a similar scheme called Rent to Own. This scheme allows the eligible individual(s):

- To rent a property, paying full market rent for up to five years.

- Have the option to buy the property once they have reached the second year, up until the five years have ended.

- Once they have applied to purchase the property, 25% of the rent is paid back and they also receive half of the increase in the value of the property since moving in, which can be used towards the deposit.

Right to Buy

Right to Buy was introduced in 1980. If you are a tenant renting a property from your local council, you may be eligible to buy the property at a discount. The criteria may differ between boroughs, but generally speaking:

- The property must be your main residence and your only home.

- You have a contract with the landlord and are, therefore, a secure tenant.

- You have no financial debt legal cases against you.

- You do not share communal spaces, or the kitchen with other people outside of those that live with you.

- You must be a tenant for a total of at least three years, even if it is not a consecutive three years.

The discount increases depending on the number of years you have been a tenant. The maximum discount is £84,200 outside London and £112,300 in London. It is also good to note that if you are obtaining a mortgage, the discount you receive with the Right to Buy scheme can be accepted by most lenders, as the deposit for the purchase of the property, which can be a great advantage of using the scheme.

You are able to sell the property at any time; however, the following applies if it was bought under the right to buy scheme and you decide to sell:

- In the first year, the entire discount has to be repaid.

- In the second year, 80% of the discount must be repaid.

- In the third year, 60% of the discount must be repaid.

- In the fourth year, 40% of the discount must be repaid.

- In the fifth year, 20% of the discount must be repaid.

- After five years, you can sell the property and you will not be required to pay any of the discount back.

Furthermore, under this scheme, if, within a 10-year period, you decide to sell it, the landlord must have the first refusal, meaning that you must offer the property back to the landlord. To apply for this scheme, you must complete the application form; RTB1 notice and the landlord should respond within four weeks.

However, the time period for a response is extended to eight weeks if the person has only been a landlord for three years. The landlord will then put forward their offer, and if they agree to sell, it will include details about the property, any associated charges, the value of the property, and how the discount will be calculated. You will then have 12 weeks to accept or decline the offer.

It is also good to note that some local authorities state that once your application is being processed, they will only do repairs to your property that they are legally obliged to do. Any other improvements will not be carried out whilst your application is current (in the process).

The Right to Buy scheme is available in England but no longer available in Scotland and Wales, and can be another opportunity to get on to the property ladder.

Lifetime ISA

Lifetime Individual Savings Account (LISA) is a government incentive for first-time buyers who wish to create a savings pot for their first home, and those who wish to save for the future. To qualify for opening this type of account, you must be between the ages of 18 to 40. You can save a maximum of £4,000 each year up until the age of 50 and the government will add a 25% bonus each year, which will be a maximum of £1,000 per year.

To ensure you do not incur a 20% withdrawal charge, you must withdraw the money only if you are buying your first home, or you have less than 12 months to live due to becoming terminally ill, or if you are over 60. The following criteria apply if you are using a Lifetime ISA towards a deposit for your first home:

- The purchase price of the property must be no more than £450,000.

- You must use a licensed conveyancer or solicitor for the purchase and the Lifetime ISA provider will transfer the funds to be handled for the purchase.

- You can use the Lifetime ISA to purchase of a property once the account has been opened for a period of 12 months or more.

- You use a mortgage to buy the property.

Note that if you are buying the property with someone else that has a Lifetime ISA, they will also be able to utilise the same benefits and can, therefore, use their savings and bonus from the government towards the purchase of the property.

Using a Mortgage

Unless you are a cash buyer i.e. you have the cash to pay for a property outright, it is likely that you will seek to apply for a mortgage. A mortgage is an amount you will borrow from a lender for an agreed amount of years and is secured against the property you purchase. Therefore, if you do not keep up with your mortgage payments, your property may be repossessed, meaning that the lender will be able to take possession of the property.

There are a range of different mortgages which I will go into further detail about, however, there are also certain actions that will be taken into consideration as part of your mortgage application.

The Property Process

Check your documents are up to date

As part of the mortgage application, the lender will need to prove your identity. You must check whether documents such as a passport, driving licence and any other official identity document or certification are valid, and where necessary, have up to date information such as your current address for the application. Ensure you can provide other required documents such as three months' bank statements and utility bills which include your correct name and address.

Credit Scores

Credit scores are created by Credit Reference Agencies and they collect and compile data on an individual's financial behaviour. The three Credit Reference Agencies that lenders use to gain this information are:

1) Experian
2) Equifax
3) TransUnion

They will use at least one. The data provided by the Credit Referencing Agencies are compiled from:

Account Data

This is data that is shared showing records and behaviour of any bank accounts, utility bills, mobile phone contracts, loans, building societies, and store cards for the last six years. A default is where payments have been missed, and this is information that will be shared with the lender and may have a negative effect on your application.

Electoral Roll

The Electoral roll is a list of individuals who are registered and eligible to vote within a particular electoral borough. It has the names of individuals and their current residential address. This information helps lenders confirm your identity.

The Property Process

Searches, Linked Data, and Addresses

This information includes records of people you have a financial link with, any addresses you have been linked with, and any searches that have been carried out by any other lender you have applied to.

Court Records

This informs lenders of any County Court Judgments (CCJ), bankruptcies, Individual Voluntary Arrangements (IVA) and any other types of debt orders. This helps the lender to become aware of any debt issues. When you are at the stage of speaking to a mortgage advisor, it is important to pass on any court record information that is on your file, as they may be able to find more suitable lenders to meet your needs.

As I have previously mentioned, I like to use the *Check My File* website to keep an eye on my credit file, though there are various other websites and apps that can be used. If there is data on your file that is inaccurate, you can contact them and request it to be removed. In addition to this, an advisor may suggest avoiding using overdrafts and payday loans, cancel unused credit cards, make card payments on time, and ensure all addresses and any financial links to other individuals, such as joint account information are up to date.

Getting a Mortgage in Principle

I remember viewing properties for the first time and an estate agent asked me "Do you have a mortgage in principle?". At the time, I did not know what this was but replied "I will speak to my mortgage advisor", as I knew she would be best placed to advise me further.

A mortgage in principle is a statement that can be requested from the lender, prior to finalising your purchase, to say that they will lend you a certain amount.

Generally speaking, they are valid between 60 to 90 days and are also known as **Agreements in Principle, Decision in Principle, and Mortgage Promises.** When I spoke to my advisor about what the agent asked me, she advised that I speak to the agent informing them that the mortgage in principle will be arranged by the mortgage advisor once a suitable property is found. The reason for this advice was, should the mortgage in principle expire before I found a property, or if other searches were requested, they would show up on my credit file.

As it would appear that I was requesting mortgage lending frequently, and possibly from different lenders, the increased number of searches could have a negative impact on my ability to borrow for a mortgage. However, other individuals prefer to request it nevertheless, as estate agents may require it upfront. For some buyers, having a mortgage in principle helps demonstrate to the seller or estate agent that they are in a position to buy. Therefore, this should be a topic of discussion with a mortgage advisor. Now, let's have a look at the different types of mortgages available:

Fixed Rates and Variable Rates

The two main types of mortgages are fixed rates and variable rates:

A *Fixed Rate Mortgage* is the interest rate the lender charges that stays the same, and is normally agreed for a minimum of two years, but can be agreed for up to five years. There are also 10-year fixed-rate mortgages; however, these are not as common.

A *Variable Rate Mortgage* is where the interest rate can change.

An *advantage* of having a fixed-rate mortgage for individuals is that:

- Your monthly payments, along with the amount of interest, remain the same which is helpful for budgeting.

The *disadvantages* of individuals having a fixed-rate mortgage are:

- They cannot take advantage of having lower interest rates if the rates decrease.

- Fixed mortgages may involve paying higher fees.

- There may be an early redemption penalty, which are charges you have to pay, should you decide to leave your fixed-rate term earlier than at the end of the early redemption period, as stated in your mortgage agreement.

- You may decide to search for another lender a few months before your fixed rate ends. If not, they will be moved to the lender's variable rate, which may increase the monthly payments. A good mortgage advisor will be able to support you with this.

Some individuals may prefer variable mortgages, and therefore, monthly payments can change.

Repayment Mortgages

With a repayment mortgage, the monthly payments go towards paying both the interest and mortgage loan. At the end of the mortgage term, you will have paid off the mortgage. It is good to note that there is a difference between the *fixed interest rate term* and the *mortgage term*. The fixed interest rate term refers to the time period for the fixed interest rate mortgage payments; for example, two years.

The mortgage term refers to the length of the time period that the mortgage lender will loan the money, for example, 25 years. Though the mortgage term may be 25 years, you may not have to stay with the same lender for the whole term and may be able to switch lenders to help manage your payments, though this should be discussed with a mortgage advisor.

Interest Only Mortgages

Unlike the repayment mortgage, an interest-only mortgage is exactly what it says. You only pay interest on the mortgage, which means your payments will be lower. However, the payments do not go towards paying off the actual mortgage loan.

At the end of the mortgage term, you will be required to pay off the total amount in full. If you have this type of mortgage and want to ensure you are paying off the mortgage loan, lenders will normally allow a percentage of overpayments to be made, so you can increase the amount you pay on your set monthly mortgage payments, although you are not obliged to do so.

Standard Variable Rate mortgages (SVR)

Lenders have their own standard variable rate and the freedom to set their own level of interest rate, so it will not necessarily be linked to the base rate of the Bank of England. The standard variable rate mortgage is what you are moved on to once your fixed interest rate or any other deal you have on your mortgage ends. Part of the payment will go towards the interest and partly towards paying the mortgage loan.

It is good to note that if the lender decides to increase your interest rate, your payments will also increase as a result. You need to be aware that you will pay more towards the interest, rather than paying the mortgage, so paying more does not necessarily mean paying off your mortgage quicker with SVR. A good mortgage advisor can provide further advice on SVR's.

Discounted Rate Mortgage

The rate on this type of mortgage is the amount that is set below the lender's Standard Variable Rate but can fluctuate, as the bank may choose to increase the rate of interest at any time. The discounted rate is usually offered for a set period of time, normally between 2 - 5 years. The discount may be lower if it is offered over a longer period of time, and the payments on a discounted rate mortgage can be very low.

Capped Rate Mortgages

Capped rate mortgages work similarly to standard variable rate mortgages, in the sense that the interest can increase or decrease. The difference is that the level of interest you pay will only increase to a maximum amount, due to the *cap* on it, and cannot increase any further, even if the standard variable rate increases to a higher amount than the cap. A capped mortgage deal can last between 2-5 years. You will be moved on to the lender's standard variable rate thereafter.

Tracker Mortgages

The interest rate with a tracker mortgage tracks the Bank of England base rate, which sets the level of interest banks charge their borrowers, plus a percentage. Currently, the Bank of England's base rate is at 0.1%, due to the Coronavirus, so if the interest rate on a tracker mortgage was 2%, you would pay 2.1%.

As tracker mortgages track the Bank of England's base rate, if the interest rate increases, so will your mortgage payments. It will, however, decrease if the interest rate is dropped. Some tracker mortgages also have a set minimum rate you can pay which is known as a *collar.*

Offset Mortgage

If you have savings, an offset mortgage allows you to use those savings to reduce or, '*offset*' the amount of interest paid on your mortgage.

Guarantor Mortgages

Guarantor mortgages allow an existing homeowner who is a family member (though some lenders may accept a friend), to use their home or savings as security towards the mortgage loan. This type of arrangement means that normally, a family member or friend will be putting their property at risk, as well as being liable to make any mortgage repayments if you are unable to keep up with them.

It is something you should discuss with a mortgage advisor to ensure all parties involved understand the positive and negative aspects when using this type of arrangement. There are also other factors that may affect the type of mortgage that is right for you:

Buying as an individual or with one or more people

As I mentioned previously, mortgage lenders base the amount they are willing to lend you on a number of factors, which include assessing one's income and outgoings. If you are buying a property on your own, the lender will only look at, and assess your individual income, but also other factors, such as your credit rating. The advantages of buying as an individual include the following:

- It can be a quicker process as the lender is only assessing one person.
- You can decide on your own needs and make decisions on what you are willing to compromise on when looking for properties.
- Lowers the risk of buying with a person who has potential issues on their credit file.

Buying with one or more people

The process will be exactly the same in terms of the lender doing their assessments and checks, but the process may take longer, as they have to take into account each individual's income and other factors. The advantages include the following:

- The income of each individual is combined; therefore, they can borrow more from the lender.
- As there are two sets of income, it may be easier to save for a bigger deposit.
- The costs involved in buying and owning a property can be split.

If you decide to buy with one or more people, bear in mind that this will create a financial link to that person on your credit file, so ensure that you get professional advice so that it does not affect you negatively in the future.

From a legal aspect, your solicitor may want to know you are buying the property as *joint tenants* or **tenants in common**. Most people go on as joint tenants, which, means if one owner passes away, the surviving owner(s) inherits all of the property. Buying as tenants in common allows the owners to own a fixed percentage of the property, and have the option to pass their percentage of the property to other beneficiaries stated in their will. However, seek professional, legal, and tax advice to find out which option works best for you and your future plans.

Buying if you are Self-Employed

If you want to apply for a mortgage and you are self-employed most lenders require:

- That you have a least two years of self-assessment tax returns or two years' accounts.

- That you have been trading for at least three years.

Lenders may also ask for additional information, such as future forecasts, and will assess their calculations depending on whether you are a sole trader, a partnership, or have set up a limited company. Keeping your paperwork and accounts organised will be an advantage when applying for a mortgage.

It is good to speak with a mortgage advisor to find suitable lenders if you are using this route. Raising finances are very unique to each individual's situation. Take the time to seek advice from a qualified independent mortgage advisor who can provide you with information that will help you decide which steps are right for you.

Chapter 4 – Finding your area and property

Deciding on an area was one of the biggest challenges I encountered when I started looking for a property. There were so many things to consider! However, what sped up the process was finding out about my affordability. I mentioned earlier in the book that your affordability is an estimate of what the lender is willing to offer you based on your circumstances, and which your mortgage advisor can find out for you. The great aspect of having this as your starting point is that:

- It eliminates areas with property prices that do not fall within that bracket.

- You may be able to consider areas that you may not have considered previously, as the property prices within those areas are within your price range.

Once you have this figure, you can start considering other key factors in deciding on your area.

Your Area

There are some useful questions to ask yourself when looking for an area:

Do you want to move within the area you are currently living in, or are you happy to move further afield?

For some people who know and love the area they currently live in, and it works for their current circumstances or future plans, they will most likely want to buy a property there.

Alternatively, the area may not be suitable for others, as they may not be able to afford to buy in the current area in which they live. Therefore, they are happy to move out to affordable areas where they can purchase a property within their budget. Think about what mile radius would work for you and what areas fall into that radius.

Are there any major developments happening in the area now / in the next few months / in the next few years?

This can be either negative or positive for one to consider when looking for a specific area, such as a major railway development for commuting purposes, a new motorway, or redeveloping a town centre. Consider the type of environment you want to live in. Will the changes in the area create a certain vibe such as more nightlife or more community cohesion? The potential increase or decrease in the price of properties in the area, that may happen due to the changes, must also be taken into consideration.

Does the area offer good transportation links / accessible amenities/schools?

If one of the reasons to buy a property is because of commuting or if you regularly use public transport, then ensuring there are good transport links in the area is going to be a top priority. Check the cost of public transport in the area, how much is a daily / weekly /monthly / annual ticket to areas you may travel to frequently? Consider whether you want to have accessible amenities, or would prefer an area that is more remote in the country? Are schools an important factor in your chosen area?

Do the property prices in that area work for you?

As I mentioned before, your affordability should help you answer this question. Once you know this, a really useful website that can help you decide on an area and analyse property prices is *home.co.uk/#tab-prices-and-rents*. It is also best to physically visit areas you have shortlisted.

The Property Process

As a buyer, you may be willing to commute for up to an hour and want to be close to relatives and schools for example. You may alternatively want easy access to amenities or be close to exciting upcoming developments that would enhance the area.

During my search, I made sure that I drove up and down different roads. The more I did this, I started to realise the difference in areas and what I would be looking for, which vary from street to street. I also visited my chosen area at different times of the day. This was a key part of my search because it allowed me to understand that if there was a change in the way an area felt during the day, in comparison to evenings. There are also key points you want to look for when looking around different areas which include the following:

Litter

Look at how litter is being managed in the area. Are the streets littered? Are there fly-tipping issues, where large amounts of rubbish or items of furniture are left in the streets illegally? Are there communal bins or individual bins for each household that is being well maintained? You can also look at the local council website to get more information about how litter is managed in the area.

Noise

Noise can differ in areas, depending on the time of day, which is why it is a good idea to visit during the day, and later in the evening. Is the area generally quiet? Are there busy roads, motorways, or train lines in the area that may cause more noise? Check if noise is a problem on a particular road, in comparison to other roads. I remember when I was visiting an area with a friend who was buying a property and the road seemed very quiet. However, we noticed that as we drove to the end of the road, there were noise issues, as well as anti-social behaviour.

The Property Process

<u>Parking</u>

If you drive or are likely to have family or friends visiting who also drive, parking may be an important consideration to note when visiting an area. Check for signs with parking restrictions or permit holder notices. Alternatively, there may be only one allocated space per household or flat, and other places for visitors to park. With greener, more energy-efficient cars are being produced, consider if you may want to check whether there are electric charging stations nearby. Also look out for any potential traffic issues, for example if the property is in close proximity to a school, the road may become busier during school opening and closing times.

<u>Types of Properties</u>

The great advantage of buying a property is the wide range of different properties available and this can be another factor to consider when deciding on an area. Some of these types of properties include the following:

- **Detached** – a single property not joined to another house within its own land.

- **Semi-detached** – two houses joined by a single wall.

- **Terraced houses** – houses in a row and joined by a single wall on either side.

- **End of terrace** – a house at the end of a terrace that is joined by a single wall.

- **Bungalows** – normally detached single-storey properties or have a room in-built into the sloping roof space.

Flats are normally leasehold properties. The different types of flats are:

- ***Purpose Built Flats*** – These are flats that are built specifically to be used as flats.

- ***Flat Conversions*** – An example of this is where a house with two levels are split so that each level has its own self-contained flat.

- ***Maisonettes*** – These properties are flats that have their own front door entrance, rather than an entrance door into the main building.

- ***Apartments*** – These are typically marketed as more luxurious types of flats.

Leasehold / Freehold

These terms ***leasehold*** and ***freehold*** were words I had come across but didn't understand the difference, until a friend of mine bought a flat. I bought a house and saw the difference for myself!

When I bought my first house, it was a freehold property, meaning that I owned the freehold and the land on which the property was on. However, the flat, which my friend owned, was a leasehold property. This meant that the owner did not own the land on which the property was on; therefore, ***leased*** the property from the freeholder for a number of years. In addition to this, they had to pay fees to the freeholder. This included a service charge to cover maintenance of the building, such as cleaning, gardening, repairs, and maintenance of communal areas, and ground rent which is a rental payment to the freeholder.

Due to government legislation in Scotland, leasehold properties have been effectively ended, and therefore, leasehold properties apply to England, Wales and Northern Ireland, although in Northern Ireland, you can opt-in to buy the freehold by applying to Land & Property Services and paying the costs involved, which is an administration fee and about nine times the annual ground rent.

There will always be pros and cons for each of these properties that you should consider before buying. For example:

- Buying a freehold house may mean compromising on not having a beautiful view overlooking the surrounding area in a leasehold high-rise apartment.

- Having lift access within a building in which a leasehold flat is located is great; *however,* if there is a maintenance issue and it is not working, climbing flights of stairs with shopping or a pushchair can be quite a challenge!

- Within a building where there are leasehold flats, it can be observed whether neighbours respect communal spaces and whether the building is clean and maintained regularly.

- There are costs in owning a leasehold property, which includes paying a monthly service charge. Furthermore, if the freeholder decides to change all the windows in every flat, this would be considered as major works. As a result, the leaseholder may be billed to contribute towards the cost of these works.

- Depending on which level the flat is situated, you may not have access to a private garden as you may with a freehold house.

These are some factors you may want to consider when deciding on the type of property you desire.

Check the length of the Lease

The lease has a range of information which includes how long you can use and live in the property. Leases under 80 years can be tricky to mortgage and expensive to extend. Always check with your solicitor and mortgage advisor to get professional advice on this. Leases can be from one year to 999 years, and if you want to extend your lease, it is advisable to use an enfranchisement solicitor.

The Property Process

<u>Understand Your Lease</u>

Leases contain agreements between the leaseholder and the landlord that are known as **covenants**. Some covenants in a lease are to ensure the property is occupied and looked after in a particular way. Therefore, it is very important to take note of the covenants in a lease.

Someone I know who purchased their flat, considered creating another room by building a wall. However, their lease stated that they must not make any additions or structural alterations to the flat without consent from the landlord. The lease also included further information about their responsibilities such as:

- Insuring the contents of the flat.

- Paying all charges due.

- Not sub-letting the property which means renting out the property to someone else, without informing the landlord and getting their consent.

- Maintaining the property internally, decorating, making sure walls, doors, door frames, ceilings, and flooring, to name a few, are in good repair.

Your solicitor or licenced conveyancer should highlight any particular concerns with the lease, such as increasing service charges or ground rent. Make sure that you understand the lease and what it entails before accepting it.

<u>Service Charges, Ground Rent and Major Works</u>

Unlike freehold properties, leasehold properties come with a range of costs. As I mentioned previously, service charges are costs towards maintaining communal areas and repairs to the building, while ground rent is paid to the landlord / freeholder.

The ground rent can be quite low. However, make sure there are no covenants where the ground rent continually rises. Service charges can also be expensive and is a cost that needs to be factored in when deciding on this type of property.

In addition to this, make sure you are aware of possible major works. Major works refer to substantial work the landlord will arrange to be carried out on the building. This could be replacing all the windows, carrying out electrical works throughout the building or roof repairs. Before carrying out any of these works the landlord or freeholder will inform you of their plans. This is information that your licensed conveyancer or solicitor should also request.

With major works, these can lead to higher bills. There was an occasion where electrical works had to be carried out within a block of flats, and leaseholders were informed and given an estimate. In the end, the final bill for each leaseholder was over £3,000 which had to be paid, although payment plans could also be arranged. Sometimes, leaseholders pay into a *sinking fund* or *reserve fund* which helps cover costs towards unexpected repairs.

Rules are in place, outlining how landlords need to manage these funds. It is also good to note that if you have to pay into these funds, they are normally non-refundable, even if you move to another property. Having unexpected bills like these can be an issue for budgeting, however, for others, flats may be more suitable, so they are willing to take on the extra costs.

Leaseholders may try to lower their costs by buying a share of the freehold if the option is available. This means the leaseholders who own a share of the freehold can take on certain responsibilities, such as maintaining the building and insuring it. They will also have the ability to make changes to lease and extend it, if necessary. This process requires a good solicitor and getting a valuation of the freehold.

Alternatively, leaseholders can control the maintenance of their building through the *Right to Manage* or appoint a managing agent to do this. Right to Manage can be cheaper than buying the freehold property. To be eligible for this, the following must apply:

- The lease must be more than 21 years from the time it was given to the leaseholder.

- Two-thirds of the flats must be leasehold.

- 75% must be residential and not used for business purposes.

- At least 50% of leaseholders are involved.

There are other responsibilities, such as setting up a company and dealing with any costs involved in the Right to Manage process.

Off-Plan / New build vs Pre-Owned

According to the Statistical Data Gov UK website (**www.gov.uk**) in England alone, there have been 169,020 new homes built between 2018-2019, due to the need for more homes. However, the decision on a new home or pre-owned home will come down to preference, finances, and future plans. I tend to look for pre-owned homes that need refurbishment. Although that may not be the case for you and your circumstances, as being able to move straight into a property may be more appealing.

Off-Plan

If you decide to buy off-plan, you are committing to buying a property that is not completed, or the construction of the property has not commenced. Some of the reasons why this could be a good option are:

- You will be the first person to own a brand-new home.

- You can have some input on where you want to be located, for example, an end plot. You can have a say in the layout, fixtures, and fittings in the property, as it has not yet been built.

- You may get a discount when buying off-plan.

- Your warranty provider normally covers your deposit should the firm become insolvent and therefore unable to start or complete the build of the property.

- You may be able to purchase through a government incentive such as ***Help-to-Buy***

However, if you decide on this option, there are some potential disadvantages that should be taken into consideration:

- You are effectively buying something you haven't seen, and therefore, taking a risk, as it may not turn out the way you expected.

- This option can be trickier to mortgage. For this reason, it is useful to consult a mortgage advisor.

- There could be delays in building the property for many reasons; the length of delay could affect your mortgage offer, as they are valid for a certain period of time.

- Once you have paid a reservation fee, some developers expect to exchange contracts and pay a deposit of 10% (though it can be higher) within 28 days.

- The developers may encourage you to use their solicitors and mortgage advisors, however, you are not obliged to do so. It is a good idea to have comparisons, seek independent advice and ensure whoever you instruct will consider your plans for the future.

- If the property has not been built well, you may have additional problems to rectify.

In addition, there is a possibility of the property value increasing or decreasing between the time you pay the reservation fee, and the property being built.

A friend of mine who bought her flat which was new at the time said one of her neighbours bought her flat off-plan and paid £135,000. Once the development was completed, my friend bought her flat for £100,000 and her other neighbour who was one of the last people to buy in the development, paid £88,000!

There was a massive difference in their purchase prices. On the other hand, my mortgage advisor knew of someone who bought a property off-plan. Then, due to the significant price increase in the area, the person had a good amount of equity in their property, so there can be varied outcomes using this route.

New Build

For some, once the property is built, a new build home is more appealing, as they can see a brand new with living space, fresh flooring, and new fixtures and fittings. A new build property can be great for the following reasons:

- The buyer can move in straight away and doesn't have to worry about additional works to the property.

- New builds are often linked to schemes such as **Help-to-Buy**, so the initial deposit can be a smaller percentage.

- As the property is brand new, it gives the buyer an opportunity to furnish it to their own taste.

- The buyer will normally receive a 10-year warranty for the property. In essence, if something included in the warranty was faulty or damaged, the developer will be responsible to fix it.

- If you buy a new build, the developer may include incentives such as covering the cost of stamp duty.

- Depending on the type of property you buy, it may grant you access to additional benefits, such as a concierge, communal green space, or shared gym facilities.

- New build homes are normally more energy-efficient, compared to older properties.

- You may have the opportunity to add value to the property by extending, converting the loft space or considering other options, if applicable.

Also, there are some disadvantages to buying a new build, which include the following:

- There can be issues with the quality of the overall finish. I remember visiting someone who lived in a new build property and not only were there a couple of leaks in the bathroom, but there were also issues with the kitchen that was fitted. Due to problems that may arise like this, you may decide to arrange for a snagging survey to be completed as soon as the developer allows you to access the property. They will be able to outline any issues and communicate with the developer to ensure it is rectified.

- More often, new build homes can look the same as others in the development stages. Furthermore, there may be restrictions associated with altering the structure of the property.

- The amount of space in new build properties can be limited, as developers may need to build a large number of properties within the development. Check if outdoor space or storage space is sufficient for your needs.

- There is the risk of paying a higher price for the property because it is new.

- There can be delays if the property is not fully ready, and can affect your move-in date, and potentially your mortgage offer.

- The warranty provided for new build homes may not cover everything therefore it is important read this carefully.

- Developers may encourage the buyer to use their recommended solicitors. However, it is a good idea for the buyer to compare other options before deciding to instruct a solicitor to work on their behalf. A solicitor can work towards agreeing a *'long-stop'* completion date. This is the date in which the developer must ensure the property is completed. There may also be a *'short-stop'* which is the estimated date the property will be completed. The solicitor can work on the buyer's behalf to ensure the contract is tailored to their needs and make sure their deposit is protected.

New build homes can be a great option for some people. However, it is very important to consider whether they will work for your current circumstances and future plans, particularly if you decide to use a scheme such as **Help to Buy** or **Shared Ownership** previously discussed in chapter 3.

Pre-Owned

Pre-owned properties refer to properties that already exist and are older. I love what I can find when walking into these older properties. The decor identifies the era and previous owners' choices at that time.

When stripping the wallpaper, I have found Disney characters or pencil marks on the walls with names next to them, showing the growth in height of a child who most likely stayed in that particular room. I find it interesting how you can uncover historical memories of a house! However, as with the previous options, opting to buy this type of property does have its advantages and disadvantages:

- One advantage is the **character.** Depending on when it was built, the property may have character features, such as high ceilings, original fireplaces, decorative windows, decorative arches, or original switches that you may not find in modern properties.

- Another advantage is **space.** Some older properties may have more square footage space internally and externally. They may also have bigger garden spaces, bedrooms and living spaces may be larger.

- Having the option to increase the size of the property, or add value by putting your own stamp on it, is another reason why these types of properties can be appealing for some. They may have the potential to be extended, convert the loft space into a room, or even build another structure at the end of the garden; there can be various options to consider.

- Older properties can be part of established close communities, as people have lived in the area for many years and utilise local facilities, such as green spaces and social spaces including local community centres and pubs.

- As the property may need work, you have more opportunities to negotiate on the price to factor in additional costs.

There are some **disadvantages** that should be considered before buying this type of property which include the following:

- As these properties are older, they have suffered more wear and tear; therefore, when a survey is carried out, or if you are starting a refurbishment, you may encounter problems that can be costly to repair. Always have a contingency budget for potential unexpected costs.

- Older properties can be more expensive to maintain due to their age.

- They may have older heating systems or single glazed windows, which is likely to make them less energy efficient. Therefore, you may have higher bills and have to factor in the cost of upgrading these.

- The property you want to buy may be a listed building. Listed buildings are protected buildings that are considered to be of national importance, due to historical interest or special architecture. There will be restrictions on what can be changed internally and externally, and consent for changes must be applied for by the owner. Listed buildings can be found at: **https://historicengland.org.uk/listing/the-list/**

- The buying process may take longer, as there are many people involved. For example, the seller may be buying another property, whilst trying to sell their own property.

- There may be occasions where the size of the rooms is disproportionate. For example, the bedrooms and living room may be spacious, however, the kitchen may be very small. If this is the case, consider whether this can be rectified by refurbishing or extending the property following the correct procedures and regulations.

Buying at an Auction

Buying at an auction is not a suitable option for many. This is because there are terms and conditions when using this route. Some properties sold at auctions may have additional issues and it may be very difficult to secure a mortgage.

There may also be substantial damage that can be very costly to repair. Buying at an auction means you have to proceed quickly because if your offer is accepted on the fall of the hammer, you become the legal owner of the property. Normally, you have to pay a non-refundable 10% deposit on the day and ensure the purchase is completed normally within 28 days.

In addition to this, you will also need to pay any other fees associated with the auction house and sale of the property. It is also a good idea to get a solicitor to check the legal pack. For those who use this route and are fully prepared for purchasing, it can be an opportunity to find a suitable property.

Whether it is a house, flat, cottage, lighthouse, or even a castle that you may want to live in, consider your options. **There is no right or wrong property**. Speak to key people in your team, arrange to visit the different properties you have shortlisted to see the difference for yourself, and have a feel for whether or not it will suit your needs and expectations.

There will also be differences in prices, depending on the type of property you want. It may also be easier or more challenging to mortgage. Speaking to other key professionals will contribute in doing your due diligence and making decisions about an area.

Letting Agents

One top tip when starting your due diligence is speaking to local letting agents in the area, preferably an agent that only offers a lettings service and is not affiliated to, or has any links with a sales estate agent service, particularly if you are buying a property for investment.

Letting agents can provide information, including what type of properties are in demand within a certain area, and what roads are desirable and less desirable, because of nearby motorways and industrial areas, for example.

Letting agents are a great resource and are willing to provide this information. More so, if you are buying for an investment, you may be someone who could potentially use their services, so ultimately it is a win-win situation.

Estate Agents

I previously spoke about estate agents and their roles in the property buying process. When deciding on an area, it is useful to build a rapport with several estate agents.

The Property Process

Speak to estate agents and explain what type of property you are looking for, what area, the number of bedrooms you desire, and any other key information if you desire off-road parking or a large garden.

They are likely to request your contact details and will add you to their mailing list and send properties of your interest. Aim to keep in regular contact with them, as this helps to build a good relationship and may make you aware of properties before they go on the market. A good estate agent will have local knowledge about the area.

Online Research

Doing online research is a great way to get started when looking for a property. Though it is important to carry out this type of research, ensure that you go out and visit areas and use and compare the information that you have found. When assessing property values, there is a big difference between the price of a property that is *selling* and the price of a property that has *sold* (see Making Offers – Chapter 7). There are websites I've listed below that are useful for online research:

Property Tracker

Property Tracker is an extension that can only be used with the Google Chrome browser. Once installed, this useful tool tracks the historical changes in prices of properties advertised on Rightmove. There are colour-coded arrows that display next to the price of the property; red to show an increase since being listed, blue to show the price has remained the same, and green to show a decrease in price. This is helpful in understanding how long the property has been on the market, what price the seller may be trying to achieve, and whether they would consider lower offers.

Nethouseprices

Nethouseprices is a website that allows you to search for properties on particular roads and areas.

When the list of properties is generated, Nethouseprices allows you to see the history of the property, including if it has been sold previously.

It also includes price changes to the property and when the property came on the market. This information is useful in helping to make a decision on your final offer, negotiating and checking if the estate agent is providing the correct information. It is a good idea to document the information gathered on a spreadsheet.

Street Check

Street Check is a useful website that generates various information about a specific area. You can type in the name of a specific road or a postcode. The first tab provides you with a summary of the area. The second tab includes information about the number of properties sold, what price they were sold at, and the different types of properties within that road or postcode.

There are tabs with further information and people in the area, including age groups, working status, educational levels, cultural backgrounds, and crime statistics. This can be used as a great comparison tool when visiting areas, as well as gaining information about the areas you may be unfamiliar with.

Home.co.uk

Home.co.uk is a website that is great for accessing a variety of information, such as name and contact details of estate agents and letting agents within an area, comparables of different types of properties in a selected area, and comparing sold prices.

Land Registry

Land Registry is a non-ministerial government department that was created in 1862 and holds records of registered ownership of properties and land.

You can use the land registry to search for title deeds, but can also be used to check sold prices of properties in the area. The website **http://landregistry.data.gov.uk/app/ppd** provides information on sold prices.

You can enter the full address on the website, select the type of property it is, and select *'all'* for the last question, which asks *"how many results?"* This will then generate a list of sold prices and the dates of which the property was sold, which is a great tool as part of your research and negotiation on your purchase price.

Rightmove and Zoopla

Two of the main property search engines that are used when looking for a property are Rightmove and Zoopla. They include filters such as maximum purchase price, number of bedrooms, and area radius. They have useful calculators, potential cost breakdowns, maps, agents contact details, as well as the option to set up alerts for new properties that come onto the market. *On The Market* is another property search portal that offers the option to set up alerts for *'new and exclusive'* properties advertised 24 hours or more, before they are listed on Zoopla or Rightmove.

Council Tax Band

It is useful to find out the cost of council tax in an area, as it can be a significant cost to factor in. There is a useful website called Council Tax Finder; **www.counciltaxfinder.com** where you can enter the postcode of your chosen area and it lists the yearly charges, the council tax band, and which financial year the charge relates to for each property on that road.

As I have mentioned earlier, you may also carry out online research for tradespeople, if the property you are buying requires refurbishment. You may start with getting recommendations from others. Then move on to doing further research online. It is always useful to get at least three quotes.

The Property Process

Arrange a visit to properties you want to consider purchasing with your tradesperson, as they will be able to see what essential refurbishment works need to be carried out and how much this will cost.

It is important to keep your end goal in mind and let the tradesperson know exactly what your plans are. Ask the tradesperson to provide you with a detailed quote including a breakdown of materials, labour costs, and an estimated timescale for the works. When considering any works, think about the future – Will this add value to my property? Will the property be able to meet my needs in three to five years' time (if you are planning to live there long-term)? See the section on tradespeople in this book for more detailed information. Finding the right area can be time-consuming, but is also an exciting part of the process.

Chapter 5 – Viewing Properties

I have to admit; this is my favourite part of the process! I love looking around properties, seeing the different styles, sizes, scope for changes to add value, changes to the layout, and how different furnishings give the property a certain feel. In addition to this, I enjoy meeting owners and agents, talking about the property, the area, and sometimes, aspects of their own life. Starting with research is great. The next step is to arrange viewings so that one can compare the research done, to the actual market.

If you are buying with others or your family, get them involved. I have on occasions taken my children with me when going on viewings. My eldest child helped me to take photos of the property; (always with the permission of the agent or seller). My youngest child enjoys having conversations with the seller or agent.

Another benefit of bringing your family / other people along to viewings is outlined in this example: A friend of mine put in an offer on a property they were hoping to buy. The seller, having met their children accepted the offer over another individual who put in a slightly higher offer, because they built a rapport with them, and also the property had a lot of sentimental value.

As a result, the seller wanted a family to move into the property, and mentioned that their children would get on well with the other children in the neighbourhood. Having other people attend viewings can also be great in offering an extra pair of eyes when looking around and providing a second opinion.

When starting to view properties, having a checklist is useful, ideally on your phone, as taking a physical checklist to a viewing may take away the element of building rapport with the agent or seller if you have a long list and looking at it from time to time. Always carry your phone to take photos after ***seeking permission*** from the agent or seller. A tape measure and torch are also useful resources. Endeavour to view a certain number of properties that it is manageable. Allow yourself time to review, compare, and possibly assess whether there are aspects of your ***property wishlist*** that you may be willing to compromise on.

The way viewings are currently being conducted at the time of writing this book has changed, due to the present pandemic; and are either being carried out online, or face-to-face with strict procedures. You get more from going to visit a property. However, if you only view it online, the majority of the checklists below will still apply. Here are a few points to note when viewing properties:

Interior Walls

Look for any cracks whether large or small. All properties have a degree of movement at some point. However, depending on the size of the cracks, it may indicate structural issues or subsidence – this is where the ground under the property falls or sinks gradually, and therefore, cracks appear due to the pressure placed on the structure of the property. Look for stains or mould on the interior walls. Is there plaster coming off the walls? Is there loose wallpaper? Does it feel damp when touched? Are the skirting boards along the bottom of the wall damaged? This could indicate a range of different issues and may need further investigation, such as the images below:

The picture on the **left** is an example of a damp wall.

(**Source:** https://www.dreamstime.com/white-wall-cracked-paint-rain-water-leaks-wall-causing-damage-peeling-paint-image120851508).

The picture on the **right** is an example of a damaged skirting board.

(**Source:** https://www.dreamstime.com/wood-skirting-board-became-swelling-water-damage-incident-occurs-image145414999).

Flooring

Are there any visible holes? I've visited properties where the staircase had been removed, and you could see the top floor of the property! Does the floor dip or slope in places? When you walk, does it feel springy? Are there any loose floorboards? Are there any floorboards that are crumbling, or can you see small holes in the floorboards? This could be a sign of woodworm. A good surveyor will be able to identify this and recommend the best course of action.

Ceilings

Does the ceiling have polystyrene tiles? These are a fire risk and it is best to get advice on these. Are there any cracks? Does it have any bulges? Is the coving damaged? Are they any bits of plaster hanging off from the ceiling? Can you see any holes? A good surveyor will tell you if the ceiling has any *asbestos*. Asbestos fibres can be a concern because of the reports of how it damages people's health. A good surveyor will be able to tell you if it is a cause for concern, as it will depend on whether the ceiling is undamaged, how much asbestos may contain, and whether it needs to be removed by a specialist.

Loft / Attic

This is where having your own torch can come in handy. Although there may already be a loft ladder installed, always seek permission from the agent or seller to go into the loft space. It is normally a lot easier if the property is empty, as it is less intrusive. It is good to look for any gaps in the roof space, and whether the timber is in good repair. In addition to this, check if it is well insulated.

Windows

It is important to check windows during a viewing, as replacing them may be a significant cost, depending on the type and number of windows, and if they are single glazed or double glazed.

Single glazed; though they can be cheaper, may not insulate or retain heat, as well as double glazing would. Subsequently, this can lead to the property being less energy efficient, resulting in potentially higher bills in colder months.

Double glazing can be more energy-efficient and minimise external noise, which you may want to consider, depending on the location you are buying in. Check what types of frames are used. Are they PVC, aluminium or timber and are they in good condition?

Check for any cracks in the frames, mould, or fungus growth. Ask for permission to open the windows and see if they open easily, and check if they are lockable or have any other defects.

Radiators

Note how the rooms are being heated. Are there radiators powered by a gas boiler system or are they electric heaters? This will affect bills, energy efficiency, and potentially have to be a cost to consider if replacing. If you decide to replace them, it is advisable to speak to a plumber about the size and number of the radiators and the BTU (British Thermal Unit) required.

This is important so that rooms in the property are not too hot or too cold.

Boilers

Have a look at the boiler, if there is one. Where is it located? Could it be in the loft space? What type of boiler is it? A back boiler (see picture on page 75), a conventional boiler with a hot water cylinder, or a combi boiler, for example? Has the boiler been serviced annually?

Depending on the age and type of the boiler, you may want to replace it to make it more energy-efficient. Are there any visible leaks? Is it in safe working order? Is there a warning sticker that states 'do not use'? If there is a hot water cylinder, where is it located? Boilers can cost thousands to replace and is a cost that will need to be factored in.

My own picture of an old-fashioned back boiler

Pipes

All pipework may not be visible, as it some may be placed under flooring, however, check if any visible pipework is in good repair. Can you see any leaks? It is also worth checking if any pipework has been capped off – this is a cap put on the end of a pipe to stop leaks, or alternatively used for pipes that are no longer in use.

Has plastic or copper pipes been used in particular rooms? Where is the stopcock located? This is the valve used to turn off the water supply to the property.

Fireplaces

If there is a fireplace, where is it located, and is it connected? What type of fireplace is it? If you wish to reinstate it as a working fireplace, it is best to get specialist advice from a qualified professional.

Electric Supply

Checking the electrics is very important during viewings. As with the pipework, not all electric wires will be visible, as they are run under floorboards and walls. Look for the main source of electric supply. Is it in working order, or does it need modernising? Are there any exposed wires? Are there a large number of wires being fed through to a particular place? If the supply is quite old, you may need to consider rewiring the property and factor the cost in, as it can be very expensive.

The picture on the **left** shows old electrics.

(**Source:**https://www.dreamstime.com/old-electricity-meter-circuit-breaker-wooden-substrate-inside-room-under-artificial-lighting-electrical-safety-image190454534).

The picture on the **right** shows a modern electrical fuse board – this is my own photo of a modern fuse board.

Lighting

Look at the lighting in a property. It may be difficult to see if the lighting is sufficient for the room when viewing the property during the day. However, it is good to check if it is in working order. What type of lights are they? Are they pendant lights? – (lights that have bulbs at the end of wires or a fixture), spotlights set into the ceiling or strip light bulbs? Are there any visible loose wires?

Sockets

Going through the experience of refurbishing a property made me realise how important it was to have the correct number of sockets and that they were in the right locations. Are the sockets in the property located in accessible places? There may be sockets behind doors or extremely close to other appliances, which you may see during a viewing. Some may have been fixed to skirting boards in older properties. Are there sufficient sockets in the property and are they overloaded with plugs, which could be a potential fire hazard? Where are the telephone and TV points located?

Switches

Older switches may mean older electrics, so have a look at them. For some buyers, the older switches are aesthetically appealing and are added features in a property. A qualified electrician will be able to advise you further.

Baths

Are there any bathrooms in the property and if so how many? Does the bath have any visible cracks, mould, or other damage to taps or plugholes? Is the side panel of the bath in good repair? What material is the bath made from, is it steel, cast iron or an acrylic bath for example? Does the colour work aesthetically for what you want to potentially create in the property? Check the seal around the bath. Is it damaged or is there mould? If there are tiles, check them and the surrounding grout to see if they are in good condition.

Toilets

With some older properties, historically, the toilet was built at the back of the property. Therefore, it is good to check where the toilet(s) are located and if there is more than one in the property? Is it in working order? Is there any damage or leaks?

Showers

If there is a shower in the property, what type of shower is it? Is the shower over a bath or a stand-alone? Is it an electric shower? Is there any damage to the showerhead or pipework? Are there any leaks? Check the shower screens for mould, loose seals, and any damage.

Basins

What type of basin is in the property? If it is a freestanding pedestal basin, check for any cracks, chips, or leaks. If it is a wall hung basin with a cupboard, check if the cupboard doors are in good repair. Check for any signs of leaks inside the cupboard, for cracks, and look at the taps to see if they are damaged.

Alarm Systems

Are there smoke alarms and carbon monoxide detectors? This should be checked as a priority when looking around a property. Is the smoke alarm hard-wired or battery operated? Where is the carbon monoxide detector located? Is there a heat sensor? Check if the property has a security alarm system. Is it in working order and does the agent or seller know the code? There was an occasion where I went to view a property with an agent and they had the incorrect code for the security alarm system. It went off throughout the whole viewing, and eventually, the seller had to come and reset it!

Doors

Check the doors as you move from room to room. Do they move easily? Are they on their hinges? Are they fire doors or have other doors been fitted? Are the handles on the door in working order? If there are any locking mechanisms on the door, do they work? Look out for any damage to door frames or architraves. Are the doors warped? This could indicate problems with the seal or be caused by excessive heat or moisture.

The Property Process

Staircases

If the property has a staircase, take note of how it feels walking up and down the stairs. Are they very steep? Can you feel any loose joints? Where are they located in the property? Is there a handrail, and is it secure? Are there any broken or damaged spindles? Is the newel post and spindles low in height? The newel post is the post at the top and bottom of the staircase to support the handrail. In order to meet building regulations, staircases need to be a certain height and width for safety reasons. A good carpenter will be able to advise further.

Unusual Smells

As you are going around the property, take note of any unusual odours. I remember viewing a property where there was a strong whiff of air freshener as I came in. However, as the viewing went on, I started to smell the musty scent of damp and realised that the air freshener had been used to disguise the smell.

There are also factors you should check on the exterior of the property, which include the following:

Guttering

Have a look up at the guttering. What material is it made from? UPVC? Concrete? Are there any leaks? Is it free of any debris, or are there blockages? Is there any other visible damage to the guttering? Are the fascias in good repair or do they look damaged?

Roof

Looking at the roof externally from the ground is useful. Can you see any loose tiles? Is it bowed in places? Does the chimney stack look as if it is leaning, or is there any other damage? Are there any flat roofs on the property? Has the flat roof been replaced recently? Is there any vegetation growth or damage to the flat roof?

Garden

A garden can be a big priority on a buyers list, so it is important to access the garden area during the viewing, if possible. Is the garden clean and tidy? When looking from upstairs, are the neighbour's gardens clean and tidy? Are there any trees in close proximity to the property? Could the roots potentially cause damage to the property? Is the fencing in good repair? Is the fencing or vegetation in the garden organised in such a way that you are able to distinguish the boundaries of your garden and that of your neighbours? Check that this particular plant (Japanese Knotweed) is not in the garden or the surrounding area of the property:

- Japanese Knotweed

  Japanese knotweed originates from Japan and was historically brought to the UK during the Victorian times, as a decorative plant, to provide stability to railway embankments.

  It is a very intrusive weed that grows rapidly and has distinctive reddish bamboo-like stems. An internet search will provide further information. Due to the nature of this weed, it can severely affect the value of a property, make it difficult to get a mortgage on the property, and can negatively affect the resale value.

  You may also be in breach of the law if it spreads from the property to other areas and so you may need to factor in the cost of professional removal of this weed.

Driveway

If there is off-road parking outside the property, look for any cracks or loose paving slabs. Is there a slope and drainage channel that is in good repair? Is the width of the driveway suitable for one or more vehicles?

Brickwork

Is the external brickwork of the property in good repair? Are there any damp stains? Are there any cracks? If the property has been rendered, is it in good condition? Has any render fallen or chipped away?

Is there any opportunity to add value?

Look at the size of the outside space. Does the property have the potential to be extended? Have neighbouring properties along the road been extended? This may give an indication as to whether the property could get planning permission for this, (though it is never guaranteed) and the correct procedures will have to be followed.

You may add value through permitted development where you do not require planning permission for certain changes or improvements, though it is always best to confirm this with the local authority and a qualified surveyor.

Gates

Is there a front gate or side gate entrance to the property? Is the gate on its hinges and in good condition? Is there a locking mechanism? Is it safe and secure?

External Pipework and Drains

Check the external pipework for any damage. Check the pipework points towards the correct drainpipe where necessary, and not somewhere unusual. Make sure that when the water is running, it runs to the correct drain. During a refurbishment I was managing, the water from the shower should have gone directly down into the waste pipe, however, because it was damaged, it had spilt outside of the pipe.

The builders working on the project jokingly offered to keep it as a water feature! Nonetheless, it was good to run the water, so the problem was seen and rectified. Check if there is a visible manhole cover in the garden. If not, has something been built on top of it?

As you can see, there can be a lot of factors to take into consideration during a viewing, but it does not need to be overwhelming. Take your time to look around the property, as it will be a big financial commitment to take on. What can also be helpful, is viewing the property more than once, as this may allow you to look for things on your checklist that you may not have looked at in detail on the first viewing.

Chapter 6 – Speaking to Agents and Sellers

A large part of finding a property involves talking to people, and building up rapport with estate agents and sellers, who can also be referred to as vendors. I have discussed the different types of estate agents that you may come in contact with when booking viewings, and the importance of taking your time during viewings. Another key factor is asking questions to gather as much information as possible before making a final decision on an offer.

<u>Questions to ask</u>

The questions asked during a viewing may differ slightly, depending on the type of property and whether the viewing is with the estate agent, the seller, or both the agent and the seller. Asking questions will help in making an informed decision about whether a property is right for you if the research carried out correlates with the information given, and whether you decide to make an offer on a property. Below are some useful questions to ask:

<u>How long have you lived in the area?</u>

This is a great question to if you are viewing the property with the vendor as it helps to build rapport. The vendor may talk about how the area has developed, why they originally moved there, whether they have friends or relatives in the area, and tell you about surrounding amenities. Some vendors may go as far in talking about changes they've seen or they've experienced in the area, which can also be very useful information.

Alternatively, if they have lived in the area for a short period of time, unless there is a key reason for selling, such as relocation for work, you may want to ask about this and have a discussion to find out the reason for moving so soon.

The Property Process

<u>What is the WI-FI / mobile reception like in the area?</u>

Internet connection is an important consideration for many buyers, as it is used widely in everyday life. Find out if there are any interruptions in connection and whether the connection is slow or fast. Are there particular times of the day where the connection is stronger or weaker? Are there hotspots in the property where the connection is better? Have a look at your mobile phone – are you able to get a strong signal?

<u>Why is the vendor selling?</u>

There are many reasons why someone decides to sell a property. The following reasons could be to upsize, to downsize, divorce, to relocate, or due to probate – this is where someone has died, and the executor(s) have decided to sell the property from the deceased estate and the proceeds of the sale are distributed among the beneficiaries. Understanding why someone decides to sell gives you an insight as to how quickly they may want or need to proceed.

It can also give an indication as to whether they will accept a lower offer, or hold out for the highest offer. The agent may not know or want to give you this information, but it is still worth asking. Asking this question may also provide an idea of who the vendor wants to sell the property to. It may be the case that the vendor(s) are selling due to probate, for example, and finds that the property has become a financial burden. Therefore, they may be less selective about who buys the property, as they are seeking a quick sale.

<u>How long has the property been on the market?</u>

You may have already carried out your own desktop research on this, but it is a great question to ask, as you will be able to compare your own findings with the information provided on the day. If the property has been on the market for a long period, this could mean that the seller is more motivated to sell quickly.

Therefore, if you are in a position to move quickly, you can create a win-win situation. Alternatively, they may be willing to hold out for the best offer. If the property is marketed by two agents, give both agents a call. From my own experience, when I came across properties that were marketed with more than one agent, there were many reasons for this. One reason is that the seller was motivated to sell quickly, and if one agent had the property on the market for a while, the seller could put it on with another agent to gain more interest from other buyers.

Who are the neighbours?

This can help you get to know the surrounding area. The seller may tell you whether the neighbours have a family, or whether they have pets. Note: If the seller is able to tell you about a few of the people that live on the road, this can be good if you are looking for somewhere that has a community-feel to it.

Have you had many viewings?

It can be helpful to have an idea about the number of viewings that were carried out on the property. Although you will never know if the number of viewings is correct, however, it can be taken as a rough guide/estimate to understand if there are a large number of buyers interested in the property and how viewings are being conducted.

Have there been any offers put forward?

Find out how many offers have been put forward. It is unlikely that the vendor/estate agent will tell you the actual price that has been offered. However, there are a few vendors that may disclose this. This information can be vital in understanding whether others are interested in the property, and if they disclose the amount that was offered, this can give you an idea of what price the vendor is looking for. If the vendor mentions this, take it as information to consider, once the viewing is over and, when deciding whether to put forward an offer or not.

Have there been any major works done to the property?

Even though you may decide to have a survey carried out on the property, it is useful to ask this question, so that you can inform the surveyor. Major works may include structural changes, or underpinning due to subsidence. This is when the ground under the foundations of the property is not stable and had to be underpinned to strengthen the foundation. Major works like underpinning can have a negative impact on the desirability and resale value of the property and would need to be factored in when making an offer. The seller may disclose other works carried out, such as the installation of a new boiler or new bathroom.

Parking Permits

If there are parking restrictions on the road, ask about the permits, how to get them, and the cost. Find out if you receive a set number of permits, and how frequently you need to apply for them.

Questions to ask if buying a new-build property or off-plan

If you are buying a new build or off-plan, some of the questions above can apply, however, there are additional questions you can ask and will be useful for this type of purchase. These include the following:

Do you have other sites I can visit?

As the property has not yet been built, having the opportunity to view other sites will give you a chance to see the finished product of other developments they have completed.

What other developments have you worked on?

This is key in understanding the developer's track record and reputation, especially if you are buying off-plan or after it has been built. If there are neighbours in the development, speak to them as well, and find out their experiences of the developer.

The Property Process

What is included in the warranty?

If buying off-plan check if your deposit is protected should the developer become insolvent. Though new build properties come with a warranty, the warranty does not cover everything. Therefore, it is useful from the outset to understand what the warranty covers, should you need to make a claim.

Is the property freehold or leasehold?

This is information that your solicitor will request when proceeding with the legal process of buying the property. However, you should ask this question so that you will be fully aware. If they confirm that it is a leasehold property, ask about the price of the service charge and ground rent, and who is the owner of the freehold, as the developer may sell this on.

If there are problems with the property, who do I contact?

It is good to know this when problems arise, because the developers may move on to other housing development projects. Therefore, they may no longer be the main point of contact. Ask for a contact details. This will help to ensure that you understand, and are aware of who to access and how to access them.

Towards the end of the viewing, let them know you will be in touch by a particular date – the timeframe may be the same day or later, for example, depending on how quickly you need to move and secure the property. This will allow you the time to go away and assess all the information. Take your time with this part of the process. At the end of the day, you are making a large financial commitment, and it is important to check to make sure it works for your needs.

Chapter 7 – Making Offers

So, you have completed three key parts of the process so far. You have chosen your team, you have done your research, and you have viewed areas and different properties. Now, you have found a property, and want to put in an offer. Let's look at this in more detail. It is good to note at this point, that the process in Scotland is slightly different. Further information can be found on the **MyGov.Scot** website.

<u>Knowing your Numbers</u>

Before making an offer, the key is to know recent *sold* prices in the areas, because the sold prices along with taking the current economic climate in the property market into consideration, help towards influencing the property prices in the area. When doing research, you may find certain areas have a *'ceiling'* price which is the maximum price a particular property has sold for.

An example of this is where a road mainly consists of two to three-bed houses which sold for between £280,000 - £310,000. There is also a four-bedroom property located on that same road, but because of where it is located, it may not have sold for much more than the three-bedroom house. If that same house was in desirable area where the road had bigger properties, that same property may have been sold at a much higher price, for example, £400,000 upwards.

Whatever your research has shown, it is good to keep these figures in mind when making your offer. As mentioned earlier, the seller may indicate what offers have already been put forward for the property. As an example, I have put in offers that were a lot lower than previous offers from other buyers, but I did this knowing that I had done my research, factored in all other costs such as refurbishing the property and came to a final figure on that basis.

Have a maximum offer in mind. As the buyer, you may be happy to offer the asking price or slightly higher, and this may be due to your research and knowing that you can add value to the property, which in turn increases its value. Alternatively, you may want to start lower and how much you offer will depend on what will work for you, the research you have done on the area, and the current economic climate.

The offer may be 5% lower, 10% lower, or even less. If asked, you may decide to slowly increase your offer a number of times to your maximum budget, but again, only increase your offer if you feel that the figure will work for you after considering all costs such as renovation costs and other fees associated with purchasing the property.

Negotiating the purchase price can also be done if buying off-plan or new build properties. Check for similar developments nearby including sold prices, and the length of time they have been on the market. If you are buying some of the last few plots left, there may be an opportunity for negotiation. Remember that stamp duty in England and Northern Ireland may be applicable, and this will be a separate cost on top of your purchase price. The government website **www.tax.service.gov.uk** has a useful calculator you can use to calculate stamp duty.

Depending on the purchase price of the property and how you are buying it, stamp duty can be quite a significant cost to take into account when making your offer. Your solicitor will outline any stamp duty that is due. Note that the tax associated with buying a property is paid in Scotland and called **_Land and Buildings Transaction Tax_**, and in Wales, it is called **_Land Transaction Tax_**.

This can get emotional...

Making offers is an exciting part of the home buying process, but it can also be an emotional one, especially when it is a property you really want. You have considered what you want, what you are willing to compromise on, and the property you found ticks all the boxes. It becomes emotional when you start giving meaning to the property such as 'I can see myself living here' or 'I can see myself spending time with friends and family here'.

The Property Process

If you are buying off-plan or a new build property, you may feel pressured to get things done quickly, as you do not want to lose your property. It is a great feeling to find a property you like, but it is also important to approach your offers with your research and not only your emotions. Remember to stick to the offer that works for you. To get to your final offer, you would have done your due diligence, taken a lot of time to work through the other processes, and subsequently make a conscientious effort to decide on an offer that works for you, so always keep this in mind.

Emotions can play a big part in decisions for both the buyer and the seller. If a buyer makes an offer, that is lower than the asking price and the offer is rejected, they may want to increase their offer because of the emotional attachment to the property. They may also not want to risk the property being sold to someone else.

On the other hand, the seller may be anxious to sell their property as they need the funds from the sale. Therefore, they may feel emotionally pushed to accept a lower offer. Developers or estate agents may also try to encourage buyers to use their recommended service providers in an attempt to get the purchase completed quickly.

Try to avoid bidding wars. Estate agents may arrange open day viewings where the property is available to view on a certain day and within a certain timeframe, so many people can view it at once. This can lead to frantic offers being made because of the number of people and potential competition.

In these scenarios, it is important to be aware of this and not allow it to influence your final offer. It goes without saying that this part of the process will inevitably become emotional. However, it is important to balance your emotions with thorough research, so that you make an offer that works for you. Ensure you do not overpay on the price of what you believe the property is actually worth.

The Property Process

Put it in Writing

After a viewing, allow yourself time to go away and do your research. Have time to think about whether you want to make a final offer. Normally, if you decide to make an offer, contact the estate agent or seller over the phone within the time frame mentioned at the end of the viewing. Mention any things you liked about the property as well and any visible issues as these are all reasons that you have considered when making your offer. Also mention your position as a buyer.

There may be various outcomes at this stage which I will go into, but always follow up with an email to ensure your offer is put forward in writing.

You may get a Negative Response

When making your offer over the phone, take the time to pause and listen to what they say. You may receive a 'yes' which is fantastic news, and things can progress to the next step. Sometimes, they may want a bit more time to think about your offer. In this circumstance, say "that is fine; when should I expect to hear from you with a decision?" and this will need to be followed up.

If your offer is rejected, you can either go away and do research and see if it is possible to increase your offer depending on your current circumstances. You can put this forward to the seller/estate agent/developer. However, do not feel pressured to do this if it does not work for you.

As I mentioned earlier, agents may prompt the seller to request a higher offer in an attempt to achieve a better price for their client. The developer, on the other hand, is also looking to achieve a good sale price. Alternatively, you can say "unfortunately, that will be my final offer at this stage". "I will send it to you in writing, and if the situation changes, please contact me". Send an email and follow-up often to see how the sale is progressing. This option allows you to show that you are still keen and ready to proceed, as well as stay in control of your offer, which may be accepted at a later date.

A **'no'** can be deflating, especially if you like the property, which can potentially be sold to someone else. Though remember, it may only be a 'no' for now as the seller's situation may change. Therefore, they may consider the offer later down the line. If it is a final 'no', and the property is sold to another buyer, it can be upsetting, but always remember there are many other properties available and eventually one will be of interest to you.

Keeping Track of your Offers

Keeping track of your offers after viewing properties can be useful. For example, if you are viewing at least three properties in one day, you will have probably met at least one to two people - either the estate agent, the seller, or both. You may have also taken some pictures, and gathered information from the questions asked during the viewing. Imagine doing this at least three times in the day! If you're anything like me, you may forget the names of people, or which property pictures match the property you viewed!

Normally, the estate agent will provide you with a printout of the particulars of the property, including information such as photos, floorplan, and energy performance certificate. After the viewing, it can be helpful to make notes of names and any key information that you have taken away from the viewing while it is still fresh in your mind.

It is also a good idea to keep track of your offers by recording them in a way that works for you. I normally use an excel spreadsheet, but there are apps such as Home Notes App that can help too. This will enable you to follow up offers made regularly, and note any changes to the asking price, as well as any changes to the seller's situation.

Gazumping

This is another strange word that I had not heard of prior to buying a property. Gazumping is where an offer has been accepted, but when another buyer comes in with a higher offer, it overrides the initial offer. Unfortunately, this may not seem very moral, but is it legal. Therefore, it is good to be aware of it and take certain actions to lessen the risk of this happening. The following can help you to be prepared:

- <u>Have your team ready</u>

  If your mortgage advisor and solicitor are in place ready to proceed, this will help speed up the buying process. Keep in touch regularly to find out what paperwork they will need from you and keep track of how the progress of the purchase is going.

- <u>Speak to the Agent / Seller</u>

  Once an offer has been accepted on a property, it is normally advertised as SSTC (Sold Subject to Contract) which means it is still in the process of being sold, although it will not legally be sold until contracts have been exchanged. Most sellers and agents will state a property is SSTC and will normally inform other buyers of this and will not offer it to them.

  However, as some sellers may want to try and get a higher price, there may still be a risk of gazumping, as the property is not legally yours. To try and minimise this risk, you can ask them to remove the property from the market and remind them why they should choose to continue proceeding with you including not being involved in a chain, which helps to speed up the process.

- <u>Show you are serious</u>

  At this stage, ensuring that you have your proof of funds for your deposit and your mortgage in principle, will let sellers know you are keen and ready to proceed. This will give them more trust in moving forward with your offer rather than potentially considering others. Keep in regular contact with the seller/agent, your mortgage advisor, and solicitor to keep everyone updated with your progress.

- <u>Home Buyer's Protection Insurance</u>

If you want to take insurance against the risk of being gazumped, you can do so. At this stage, you may have paid for legal searches, a survey, and mortgage advisor fees. If you are gazumped, you can be left out of pocket. Having this insurance allows you to claim some of the costs for occurances such as; if the seller changes their mind, if they accept a higher offer, or if the sale falls through.

Making offers is an important part of the process and there are a number of things to take into consideration. The timeframe for this part of the process may differ for various reasons, but once your offer is accepted you can move on to the next part of the process.

Chapter 8 – Offer Acceptance

If you are buying using a particular scheme such as 'Right to Buy', you may have decided to accept the offer and are ready to proceed with your purchase. Congratulations!! Alternatively, if you are not using certain schemes, you may have to experience that anxious wait from when you put in an offer to when you get a call from the seller or agent to say your offer has been accepted. It's the best feeling ever!

As nothing is secure at this stage, do not celebrate just yet, because a lot can happen within this part of the process, depending on which route you have chosen to buy the property. If you are buying a newly built home, or buying off-plan, your property should be reserved for you. However, you will need to consider the timeframe to complete the purchase, otherwise, you risk losing your reservation fee and the property. Once your offer has been accepted, you will need to inform your solicitor who will carry out a range of searches.

The Searches

Searches may highlight things that may be of concern in the future, such as a major development in the area, or the property is in a high-flood risk area. In turn, this can affect your decision to proceed further with the sale. Following the information provided by your solicitor, you may decide to put forward a revised offer.

Bear in mind that depending on the type of concerns raised in the searches, this could also potentially affect your mortgage offer, so continue to keep in regular contact with your mortgage advisor. The searches completed by your solicitor will vary according to the type of property.

Check the list below which shows some searches that may be carried out:

- Drains and roads that will serve the property.

- If planning permission has been granted for a new build property.

- Land registry to confirm the legal owner of the property is the person selling it.

- Local authority search, which is information held by the local authority relating to the property.

- Location of public drain and water that serves the property.

- Environmental searches to confirm if you are on or near a flood-risk area, contaminated land, or water.

- If buying a leasehold property, it will include information about things such as service charges or major works.

Indemnity Insurance

Your solicitor may discuss indemnity insurance with you. Indemnity insurance is a policy that protects you from potential costly problems with a property that may have an adverse effect in the future. For example, if the previous owner made alterations to a property, but did not get planning permission, the indemnity insurance policy would cover the risk of any future legal enforcement that a local authority may make, as well as the costs incurred for this type of claim.

Once the policy is in place, it will cover the new owner, the mortgage lender (if you have a mortgage), and any future owners, though check the fine print.

Before committing to this type of insurance, check if there are alternative ways you could overcome the problem. If you decide to proceed with the policy, there will need to be a discussion about who pays. It may be decided that the buyer pays, as they are buying the property and the policy will be of benefit to them.

It may be decided that the seller pays as it may be a historical issue that the existing owner did not resolve, and the seller should therefore pay. Alternatively, it may be decided that because both the buyer and the seller have reasons to pay, the cost will be split between them. However, these negotiations may cause delays in the process.

The Survey

If you decide to have a homebuyer's report or buildings survey completed on the property, these will include photographs and a detailed report of any issues. In addition to this, the reports will include recommendations for the potential problems and if applicable a valuation of the property.

Have a discussion with the surveyor and your solicitor or licenced conveyancer and if you feel that any of these recommendations may affect the price you offered, you can go back to the seller or agent with a revised offer based on the reasons outlined in the report. The outcome of this report will also be of interest to the mortgage lender. If there are any severe issues, they may review their offer, or request that you complete some of the works prior to lending the whole amount they have agreed.

The Mortgage Lender

Mortgage lenders have strict procedures to follow when assessing and stress testing an individual's financial activity in relation to what they may be able to borrow and pay back. Finding out your affordability and having a mortgage in principle are just estimates of what a mortgage lender will offer you, and the actual figure will not be known until you start your official mortgage application.

Therefore, depending on what evidence the buyer provides and how the mortgage lender has made their assessment, there could be a scenario where the lender decides they will only offer a certain amount, and this may be lower than the amount the buyer requires to purchase the property. To try and resolve this, the buyer may have to revise their offer, discuss any other potential solutions with their mortgage advisor, or unfortunately, there is a risk of the sale falling through.

Alternatively, if things do go according to plan, your mortgage advisor or lender will confirm that the application has been successful, as they have agreed to lend the amount you need, and you can continue proceeding with the purchase. Note, any changes to the purchase price as a result of issues that arise, or following recommendations in the survey report, must be relayed back to the mortgage lender, as it is likely that they will provide the buyer with a revised offer.

The current economic climate plays a big factor. At the time I am writing this, we are currently experiencing the coronavirus pandemic. This pandemic has severely affected economies around the world and has resulted in some businesses struggling financially or having to shut down with subsequent job losses and people's livelihood and income levels being affected. Due to this, some mortgage lenders were initially not accepting new mortgage applications and put many existing applications on hold whilst assessing the situation and mitigating high-risk levels.

When they decided to reopen mortgage applications, some lenders changed the loan to value percentage, which meant that some buyers were in a position where they had to raise a larger deposit, but may not have had the means to do so. However, the government also put stamp duty reductions in place until 31st March 2021, to help significantly reduce this cost, which has helped many buyers.

This pandemic has been huge and nothing like anything many have experienced, in terms of not being able to go out unless it is to buy essential goods or not being able to see family and friends. For now, this very unusual situation we are currently in has impacted everyone including mortgage lenders. However, there can be other changes in the economy that may affect a mortgage lender's behaviour towards their lending activity and this in turn can affect the progress of the purchase of a property.

The Property Process

As so many eventualities can take place during this part of the process, it is advisable to maintain regular contact via phone or email. This will ensure that records of email conversations and the progress of the purchase are well maintained, and any issues that arise during the process, as well as any other information that is required, will be dealt with promptly.

It can be disheartening when things do not go to plan, especially when there have been cost outlays, such as a survey, conveyancing solicitor searches, and mortgage advisor fees. I have had experiences where I paid out for these things and unfortunately, lost money due to the sale falling through.

However, it is best to be aware of these risks and do your best to move quickly. Communicate regularly with everyone involved to push the purchase through and work with your team and the seller or agent to find ways to resolve any issues that come up, so that the purchase can proceed and complete. If it still ends up falling through, depending on the reason for the sale, you may want to make a complaint and can do this through various channels such as:

- The **financial ombudsman** – if you felt your mortgage advisor was at fault.

- The **property ombudsman** – if the estate agent was at fault,

- **Making a direct complaint to your solicitor or licenced conveyancer's firm, following their guidelines, or contact the legal ombudsman** – if you feel your conveyancing solicitor or licensed conveyancer was at fault.

If you do not need to make a complaint because the sale fell through due to no fault of anyone involved, remember, your end goal is to find a home. Keep in touch with estate agents and the seller, as their circumstances may change. It will only be a matter of time before you purchase the right property of your preferred choice or style.

Chapter 9 – Exchange and Completion

Exchanging contracts and completing on the purchase of a property is a huge achievement! A lot has happened for you to get to this point! Though as I have mentioned, prior to this stage, anything can still happen. Before I go into further detail about this part of the process, it is important for you as the buyer, that any issues that have been raised following the survey report, searches and subsequent recommendations are understood and actioned where necessary.

Generally speaking, the buyer needs to know that the information they have about the property has been reviewed and considered to the extent that they still want to own the property, and are therefore happy to proceed with the final stages of the purchase. Once the next stage takes place, there is no going back, so the buyer must be very clear on this. If you are buying a freehold property, you will also normally be required by your mortgage lender to arrange to have buildings insurance in place at this stage.

Exchanging contracts are completed by the solicitor or licensed conveyancer, and this is when they formally exchange contracts that have been signed by the buyer and the seller. Once this has taken place, if the buyer or the seller decides to pull out from the sale, there can be serious consequences and either party can be sued by the other for doing so. At this stage, it is normally a feeling of reassurance for both the buyer and the seller, as they know the risk of the sale falling through is virtually gone as it becomes legally binding.

Before the buyer signs the contract, it is good to check the following:

- The contract has been read thoroughly and understood – Ask your solicitor any questions if you are unsure.

- The money to pay for the contract deposit is ready – This may typically be 10% of the purchase price. Be aware if you need to transfer the money from your bank account as some banks may restrict how much money can be transferred in a day. Double-check this with your bank so it doesn't cause any delays.

- A completion date has been agreed upon and included in the contract.

It is possible to exchange contracts and complete on the same day. However, this option may not be suitable for most people, because all the relevant monies, paperwork, and removals need to be in place so that the process can happen on time. This can also create added pressure to the situation. Therefore, this option should be approached with caution. Once contracts have been exchanged, the final checks will be completed by the estate agent or seller in terms of agreed fixtures and fittings. After this, you can move on to the completion process.

Completion

This is the final stage of the process where you officially become the owner of your property! Although I have mentioned that you can exchange and complete on the same day, most buyers will choose to complete within seven to twenty-eight days. The day they choose to complete should be a weekday to allow monies to be transferred easily. Check with your solicitor if there is a cut off time to transfer monies, as some may say that if it is transferred after 3.00 pm, completion may have to take place the following day as that is their cut off point.

If you are using a mortgage lender, they will need to transfer the monies to your solicitor or your licensed conveyancer. This will be sent on to the seller's solicitor and finally transferred to the seller. Be mindful that this process may take time, so communicate with your solicitor to keep up to date with what is happening. Remember, if there are any other costs that need to be paid such as legal fees or stamp duty, this money will need to be ready for transferral.

Once the completion has taken place, you can arrange a day to collect the keys from either the seller or the estate agent. Double-check all keys are included for the windows and all the doors. They may leave useful documents relating to the property, such as warranty certificates and user manuals. Congratulations you are officially a homeowner!! Although, there is a bit more work to do...

Life Insurance

Your solicitor or mortgage advisor may mention the benefits of having life insurance in place now that you are a homeowner. The main benefit of this type of insurance is to help dependents pay off part of or all debts such as your mortgage or utility bills in the event of your death or to cover costs should you become critically ill. There are different types of cover, and you should discuss which policy will be right for you. Health and age will be taken into consideration.

Mortgage Insurance

This is a separate insurance that you may be advised to take out, as it is specifically used to pay off any outstanding mortgage debt in the event of the homeowner's death. If there is a separate life insurance policy in place in addition to this, it allows the dependants to receive this as a separate payment. Again, it is best to seek qualified professional advice to see if this would be a suitable option for you.

Creating a Will

Once you own a property, it is now your asset and considered to be part of your estate. Making a will allows you to protect your assets, outline who you wish to be legally responsible for your property when you pass away and provide a legacy for your loved ones.

Council Tax Exemption

If you are planning to complete a refurbishment on the property before you move into it, speak to your local authority to find out if they offer council tax exemptions. This is where some local authorities will allow the new owner to not pay council tax for a period of time, if they are not moving straight into the property, and therefore it will be empty. However, it is also good to note that some councils may charge a slightly increased level of council tax due to the property being empty, so it is worth checking. Before you move in, there are some key things to do in preparation for your move outlined in the next chapter.

Chapter 10 – Moving Home

Preparing to Move

Prior to this point, and during the offer acceptance process, it's a good idea to start having a clear-out of any unwanted or unnecessary clothing or other items, so that when it comes to moving, you are only taking your essential items, as well as those that are of sentimental value. This will make it less stressful when sorting out what you want and don't want, and may also lower costs potentially if you are hiring a removal company, or using a smaller vehicle to do it yourself.

It is at this time you may realise how much you have or don't have. Try to not feel too overwhelmed. Instead, see it as a time to have a clear-out or shop around for essentials. Friends and family may want to give you gifts for your new home. Remember to speak to your the relevant person in your workplace to request time off for the move. Take your time with the process and check through the following to prepare:

Packing

It is useful to label and tape boxes when packing. A helpful tip that I did when my friend was moving was to keep the clothes she was taking on hangers in bags. Once she moved, it was easy to unload, hang, and organise. You may find that some shops will give you cardboard boxes and hangers if you ask, but you may also have to buy these. When packing, double-check everything has been removed from rooms, cupboards, drawers, and even up in the attic or loft area if you have one.

Do it Yourself (DIY) or use a Removal Company

Whether you decide to hire a van, use a removal company or someone who has a van and helps with smaller moves, give yourself enough time to get quotes and book hires in advance, giving yourself enough time to pack.

The Property Process

Get Help

Many hands make light work, as the saying goes! Ask friends or family to help with packing, childcare, removing items, or to look after pets, and allocate suitable times for everyone involved. You may get help with cleaning and decorating your new home before you move in, as it can be easier if the property is empty.

To keep costs down, there are stores that sell recycled paint, (these can be tins of paint leftover from refurbishments that are either full or partly used and are resold at a discounted price). Check the **CommunityRepaint.org.uk** website for more information. A little thank you present or gesture including cooking a meal is a nice thoughtful way to show your appreciation to those who have helped you.

Utilities and Broadband Suppliers

When you went through the offer acceptance stage, the seller would have completed a property information form which would have been passed on to the buyer from their solicitor. Within this form, the seller should have listed their water, gas, electricity, and broadband suppliers if they had this information. You will need to contact these suppliers to inform them that you are the new owner of the property and whether or not you will be changing suppliers.

If the information was not provided, or the seller did not have the details, you can use websites such as **EnergyNetworks.org** or **FindMySupplier** to find out. Ask if there will be a period of time for the switch-over to the new supplier to take place, and when the final bill with the old supplier will be issued to the previous owner.

Redirect Your Mail

Having your mail redirected is a good option as it gives you time to inform all necessary providers about the change of address, as well as receiving important mail.

Royal Mail offers a redirection service for a period of three, six, or twelve months, and can be arranged through their website. Make a note of what mail is being sent to your new address so that you can inform the relevant providers. More information can be found on **royalmail.com/personal/receiving-mail/redirection**.

Inform your Landlord

If you are renting a property, you will need to provide your landlord with notice of your moving-out date by following the correct procedures as outlined in your tenancy agreement. Make a note of your final meter reading, and ensure you leave the property in a good, clean condition to have a good chance of getting your original deposit back. You may also want to take photos for your records.

Here is a list of other places/organisations/people you will need to inform:

- The local authority for council tax

- Banks and building societies

- Insurance providers

- Driving licence

- Electoral roll

- Store cards

- Credit cards

- Mobile phone provider

- Subscription/ membership providers

- Family and friends

The Property Process

Moving day!

On the actual day of moving, try to keep valuables and important documents with you or someone you trust until you have settled in. The moving-in day can seem surreal and can remain like this for the first few days, but just take your time.

Making your property feel like home is a process that will happen over time. You may decide to arrange furniture or rooms straight away, or even later down the line, transform the loft space, or add an extension. Remember, your home is your home and can be a fluid project that evolves over time.

Take time to appreciate your home and celebrate how far you have come in achieving this goal. You may want to speak to a local locksmith about changing the locks on the doors just as a precaution, as other previous owners or tenants may have keys for the current locks on the property.

Get recommendations for local doctor surgeries and dentists in the area so that you can register with them. Some local neighbourhoods have groups set up on apps such as **Next Door** which you may want to join to learn more about local amenities, suppliers, trades in the area, and getting to know the neighbours, keeping up to date with events, and what is happening in the community.

If applicable, register your child(ren) at your chosen school, or place their name on the school's waiting list if there is one. If there is a long waiting list and your child is not offered a place at your chosen school, you may want to enquire about the local authorities' appeals process and appeal a school's decision. More information can be found on the website, **Gov.uk/schools-admissions**.

If you are purchasing items for your home, you can save money by buying second hand goods on apps like Shpock, eBay, Facebook Marketplace, and even visiting second-hand furniture stores. If you are buying new items, shop around to get good deals and look online to compare prices. There are stores such as Homesense where you can find unique items for your home. Whichever route you decide to take put your own stamp on it. If it is already furnished, take the time to settle in and enjoy your new home.

Conclusion

So, the process has come to an end and it may seem that buying a property felt like a rollercoaster at times. There were sharp turns, highs and lows, and even points when you felt you had started the ride all over again! However, once you have your new property, take the time to appreciate and celebrate your achievement. Do you now have the garden you always wanted or amazing views that you always dreamed of? Are you in now living in an area that has been a perfect location for you?

I remember receiving the keys and opening the door for the first time, and the surreal feeling of knowing that I was a homeowner at last! It was an added and unexpected surprise to receive a congratulations card from the estate agent and my mortgage advisor. I can't express the joy I felt sitting down on the floor with close family, (as there was no furniture yet!), giving thanks and saying cheers to the new property!

I specifically named this book **The Property Process** because as Oprah Winfrey said:

'It's only when you make the process your goal that the big dream can follow.'

My hope is that this book allows you to have a greater understanding of the process of buying a property so that you can work towards your dream of owning one. I wish you all the best in seeking, securing, and enjoying your new property!

Cost checklist

As there are several initial costs involved in the purchasing process, here is a handy checklist of costs, though not all may be applicable:

Buildings insurance ☐

Deposit ☐

Mortgage advisor fees ☐

Mortgage lender fees ☐

Mortgage lender valuation fees ☐

Solicitor / Licenced conveyancer fees and searches ☐

Survey ☐

Stamp duty ☐

References

Adhoc Property - www.adhocproperty.co.uk

Check My File - https://www.checkmyfile.com

Community Repaint - https://communityrepaint.org.uk/

Council Tax Finder - https://www.counciltaxfinder.com/

Damp Wall Images - https://www.dreamstime.com/white-wall-cracked-paint-rain-water-leaks-wall-causing-damage-peeling-paint-image120851508

Damaged Skirting Board - https://www.dreamstime.com/wood-skirting-board-became-swelling-water-damage-incident-occurs-image145414999

Dot Dot Dot Property - www.dotdotdotproperty.com

Energy Networks - https://www.energynetworks.org/info/faqs/who-is-my-network-operator.html

Find My Supplier - https://findmysupplier.energy/webapp/index.html

The Property Process

Gov.uk - www.gov.uk

Gov.uk (statistics) - https://www.gov.uk/government/statistical-data-sets/live-tables-on-house-building

Gov.uk/schools-admissions - https://www.gov.uk/schools-admissions/appealing-a-schools-decision

Help to Buy - https://www.helptobuy.gov.uk/

Historic England - https://historicengland.org.uk/listing/the-list/

Home.co.uk - https://www.home.co.uk/#tab-prices-and-rents

Home Notes App - https://www.homenotesapp.com/

Homesense - https://www.homesense.com/home

Land Registry - http://landregistry.data.gov.uk/app/ppd

My Gov.Scotland - https://www.mygov.scot/buying-a-home/making-an offer/#:~:text=Your%20offer%20must%20be%20sent,offer%20depending%20on%20certain%20conditions

Nethouseprices - https://nethouseprices.com/properties-for-sale/

Next Door - https://nextdoor.co.uk/

Old Electrics - https://www.dreamstime.com/old-electricity-meter-circuit-breaker-wooden-substrate-inside-room-under-artificial-lighting-electrical-safety-image190454534

On the Market - https://www.onthemarket.com/

Property Tracker - https://chrome.google.com/webstore/detail/property-tracker/abgkpdjomdmemeefdefalbeogkmlmand?hl=en-GB

Rightmove - www.rightmove.co.uk

Royal Mail redirection service - https://www.royalmail.com/personal/receiving-mail/redirection

Tax.Service.gov.uk - **(stamp duty calculator)** - https://www.tax.service.gov.uk/calculate-stamp-duty-land-tax/#/intro

The Statista Research Department - https://www.statista.com/statistics/1033483/main-reasons-why-people-want-to-own-their-own-home-uk/

Streetcheck - https://www.streetcheck.co.uk/

Unbiased - https://www.unbiased.co.uk/

Zoopla - www.zoopla.co.uk

Printed in Great Britain
by Amazon